PRAISE FOR
SHARED
STRENGTH

"As the sleeping giant of the global church stirs and increasingly engages in local integral mission, the authors help us engage with the new and exciting frontiers of partnership, the Spirit's key tool for achieving the unfolding global mission of the church!"

> –**Doug Balfour**, CEO Geneva Global, Tearfund director (1995-2004), co-founder of Micah Network and Micah Challenge

"For Christians, *partnership* should be more than a euphemism for outside funding. This book provides tangible help from people whose work proves the ultimate value of church partnership as 'kingdom work'."

> –**Chad Hayward**, Executive Director, Association of Evangelical Relief and Development Organizations

"This is exactly the right book at the right time. It intelligently helps us all think about and learn how to do partnership better. And working in truly functional partnerships is the only hope for making a lasting difference in our world today. Read it and grow!"

> –**Jane Overstreet**, CEO, Development Associates International

"The majority world now dominates the numbers and, in many respects, defines the vitality of the global church. In this context, the effectiveness of East-West, North-South, cross-cultural church partnerships is central to the future of Christian witness and service. *Shared Strength* is an essential read for every missions leader, missions-minded church, and concerned layperson—an essential guide for ministry in this radically changing world."

> –**Phill Butler**, CEO, visionSynergy

SHARED
STRENGTH

SHARED

EXPLORING CROSS-CULTURAL CHRISTIAN PARTNERSHIPS

STRENGTH

Beth Birmingham and Scott Todd, Editors

Copyright © 2010 Compassion International
Published by Compassion International
Design and production by The Elevation Group and Granite Creative, inc
Rope photo © iStockphoto.com/Zocha KREMA
Background texture © iStockphoto.com/Bill Noll
Other cover photos by Chuck Bigger

ISBN 978-0-9841169-4-2
Printed in Canada
10 9 8 7 6 5 4 3 2 1

CONTENTS

ACKNOWLEDGEMENTS

The editors wish to thank the team at Compassion who enabled the hosting of the Summit as well as the production of this work—Gayle Call, Dinah Meyer, Mary Lou Elliott, and Ashley Higgins. We also thank Paul Moede and Wolfgang Riedner for wise council throughout the course of this work. Special thanks also to the staff of The Elevation Group and their associates for their work in production of this publication—Megan Rieger, Susan Miller, Karl Schaller, and Devlin Donaldson. And above all, the editors express their sincere and heartfelt gratitude to each of the leaders who shared his and her wisdom and experience, both at the AERDO Summit and within the written work of this book. May God bless you with wisdom and growth as we all continue learning how to more faithfully serve Christ.

Special thanks must go to Amanda Stillman, a graduate student in Eastern University's MA in International Development, for her work in chapter review, key-point summaries, and providing an additional set of cultural lenses on this project. Prior to starting the program, Ms. Stillman worked in the Middle East with the International Mission Board for two years. She has also lived in China and Indonesia, and she speaks Arabic, Indonesian, and Chinese. Her future interests are in development and disaster mitigation in any part of the world where God puts her, though right now she's particularly interested in Somalia.

ABOUT THE EDITORS

DR. BETH BIRMINGHAM

Beth Birmingham is an associate professor of leadership and change at Eastern University. She shares her teaching load between Eastern's School of Leadership and Development (SLD) and the PhD in Organizational Leadership program, teaching courses in leadership, nonprofit partnerships, justice, strategic thinking, human resource management, and community research. Prior to a two-year teaching sabbatical in Cape Town, South Africa (2006–2008), she served as the founding assistant dean of SLD from 2000–2006 and director of international partnerships prior to that. She was part of the development team for the Pathways to Leadership program with World Vision International, focusing on nongovernmental organization leadership development, and has been responsible for administrative and academic oversight of numerous graduate programs and organizational partnerships that make up SLD, including partnerships with World Vision International, Habitat for Humanity International, Cornerstone Christian College, English Language Institute of China, Geneva Global Inc., and Theological College of Asia, among others. Her work has taken her to more than 15 countries.

Dr. Birmingham's dissertation and research interests include value creation in nonprofit partnerships, collaborative leadership and organizational structures, and collaboration for holistic community development. In 2007 she conducted two organizational evaluations for Habitat for Humanity South Africa, a leadership program evaluation for World Vision West Africa, and has a number of other research projects and articles in progress. She has co-authored a book chapter with Eastern University colleague Stan LeQuire titled, "Green Heroes Re-examined: An Evaluation of Environmental Role Models" as part of the book *Leadership for Environmental Sustainability* (Routledge Press, 2010) and an article in *PRISM* Magazine (January 2010) titled "Half the Sky . . . and Then Some" on the plight of women and girls around the world.

Dr. Birmingham holds a PhD in Leadership and Change from Antioch University, an MBA in International Economic Development from Eastern University, and a BSc in Marketing from West Chester University. She serves on the board of Sisters in Service (www.sistersinservice.org), a nonprofit focused on strengthening the development work of women living in the hardest places in the world. She can be reached at bbirming@eastern.edu.

DR. SCOTT TODD

Dr. Scott Todd is the senior ministry advisor in the president's office at Compassion International. During his tenure at Compassion he has served as director of the AIDS Initiative, Child Survival Program, and Complementary Interventions—a set of programs ranging from disaster response to Bible distribution. Dr. Todd is chairman of the board of directors for Association of Relief and Development Organizations (AERDO) and serves on the board of Micah Challenge USA. He oversees Compassion's global advocacy efforts and represents Compassion in networks focused on missions, development, and children.

After receiving his PhD in Immunology from the University of California, Dr. Todd was a National Lymphoma Foundation Scholar at Stanford University Medical Center. Dr. Todd's medical research was funded by the National Science Foundation, American Cancer Society, and the National Institutes of Health. He is a senior author on more than a dozen scientific articles published in biomedical journals, and he holds a patent for the treatment of Hepatitis C.

A passionate follower of Jesus Christ, Dr. Todd left academic research in 2003 to join Compassion International. He believes that this generation of Christians can and, by God's grace, will end extreme global poverty.

INTRODUCTION

Globalization is more than McDonalds in Beijing or wi-fi in Kigali. Global travel has accelerated. The Internet drives myriad new communication technologies. Economies and ecologies interconnect. Global publication distributes ideas, music, and entertainment—for better or worse. MTV is broadcast in Nairobi, and Kenyan Christians are reading *The Purpose Driven Life*. Ideas and cultures are colliding. A wide host of agents fuel fundamental change in our world. Globalization is a confluence of trends that push people from diverse cultures and geographies closer together and radically changes the interconnectedness of our lives.

Riding the trends of globalization, over a million North American Christians travel internationally each year on some sort of missions trip. On top of those numbers Australians, British, South Koreans, Europeans—just about everyone engages in cross-cultural missions. They arrive in foreign places to be greeted by people with broad smiles and warm hospitality who call them "brother" or "sister." They may paint walls or dig latrines or help orphans, or perhaps they just "seek relationship." They often return home saying that they "received more than they gave"—and they probably did. Although many travelers drift back into the river of life as they know it and the evidence of their "life-changing experience" is unclear, many others return with new ideas and new intentions. Plans for supporting national Christian leaders (and their churches) hold new sway among the older paradigms of missions.

The diversity of this motivated cavalry is vast. On one end of the spectrum are hero cowboys with new strategies to save the poor. At the other end "new monastics" sell everything and move to the slums of Bangkok to seek solidarity with the poor. Most, of course, are in between these extremes and are seeking wisdom. How do we best live out our faith in a hurting world when our "neighbor" now includes the one living 10,000 miles away?

Christians hold differing opinions about the trends of missions trips. Some point to good things and new possibilities. Others have trepidation about the unknown impact. Recently some have contributed valuable insights to guide the impact and effectiveness of cross-cultural engagement. A couple of helpful books on this subject are *Serving with Eyes Wide Open: Doing Short-Term Missions with Cultural Intelligence*, by David A. Livermore (Baker Books, 2006), and *When Helping Hurts: How to Alleviate Poverty without Hurting the Poor . . . and Yourself* by Brian Fikkert and Steve Corbett (Moody Publishers, 2009).

Whether globalization of cross-cultural Christian engagement is good or bad (no doubt it has both positive and negative effects), the evidence is clear that such engagements are inevitable and increasing. It is time to shift the debate from whether all these cross-cultural trips and engagements are a good thing and begin focusing on how to influence them to be as healthy and kingdom-advancing as possible. In particular, how can these "North-South" interactions best enable the churches of the global South to fulfill their mission? And, though less-often asked, how can these interactions best enable the churches of the global North to fulfill their mission?

Birthed from these cross-cultural experiences and interactions are relationships often called partnership. The word *partnership* has become so widely used that some dub it a nonword. What does it actually mean? The overuse of the word *partnership* can lead to some serious problems. For example, when one party uses the word to mean an enduring, mutually beneficial, jointly supported endeavor to reach a shared vision or goal and the other party uses the word to mean a vaguely defined "relationship," it can create misunderstandings. In extreme situations the power dynamics of such cross-cultural "partnerships" actually bring harm—possibly threatening the dignity, initiative, or empowerment of the party with fewer financial resources.

Compassion International has a strong interest in these trends and cross-cultural relationships because Compassion is deeply committed to the church. By "committed to the church" we mean something more concrete than an ideological commitment to the abstract idea of the "global body of believers." Specifically, we see the local congregation as the real, tangible expression of Christ in community—the *ecclesia* (see *Relentless Hope*, another Compassion book release). Compassion is committed to the local church and maintains long-term partnerships with more than 5,000 indigenous churches in more than 25 countries for the shared mission of protecting and developing children. Compassion's commitment to partnership with local churches is not new. We have held this commitment for decades, and we intend to keep it for decades to come.

Yet despite that long history of commitment, Compassion still has a lot to learn about how to do partnership well. Compassion recognizes its mistakes, and the bruises of poorly managed partnerships motivate a desire to be better. Similarly, for the sake of the kingdom there is a clear need for a widespread understanding of partnership. We need an understanding of principles and practices that will help kingdom partnerships succeed.

As a part of Compassion's efforts to learn from others, Compassion was pleased to support the Association of Evangelical Relief and Development Organizations (AERDO) Summit on Excellence in Cross-Cultural Church Partnerships held in Colorado Springs, Colorado, in August 2009. Leaders from organizations with extensive experience in cross-cultural partnerships were invited. Each leader was asked to share personal experiences, key lessons, and insights gained along their journey, with an emphasis on church partnerships in particular. The goal was to learn from each other, humbly sharing mistakes as well as successes so that each of us might be more effective in the ministries to which God calls us.

We believe that the insights shared at the AERDO Summit

can serve the broader kingdom. In particular the many churches that are in the early phase of building cross-cultural relationships may benefit from the perspectives offered in this volume.

Christian organizations and churches around the world possess unique strengths, experience, and knowledge. For the kingdom to most effectively advance, these organizations and churches must work together in partnership. It is also clear that working together can be much more difficult than idealists might hope. Partnership takes work. Partnership takes skills. Partnership takes a willingness to patiently learn, communicate, adapt, and grow. The perspectives shared in this volume provide insights and principles to benefit any organization or church engaged in partnership—with a particular emphasis on cross-cultural church partnerships.

I write this while in flight to Ethiopia, where Compassion will introduce a dozen North American pastors to Ethiopian pastors and their churches. Compassion is facilitating the connection of a small number of church-to-church partnerships. That thought makes some development professionals shudder. Professionals whom I respect have told me that the idea of such connections should be avoided if not actively resisted. Yet after much prayer and significant reflection on our more than 50 years of development experience, we believe God is up to something new. And we want to be part of it. We do not want fears of history to hinder us. Instead, the possibilities for the kingdom in a new era of global connectedness inspire us. If we build these partnerships from humility, wisdom, patience, and a mutual quest for God's glory, then they could be catalysts for an epic reformation in Christianity—North and South.

On behalf of Compassion and as chairman of the board for AERDO, I wish to express my sincere gratitude to each of the leaders who shared his or her perspective, both at the AERDO Summit and in this work. The collective wisdom in these pages will strengthen the health and impact of the kingdom in both the global South as well as the North. May these pages strengthen God's people for works of service, and may the new global connectedness of churches fuel a movement that honors Jesus Christ. May the nations hold His name in high esteem. And may His people be tireless participants in God's redemptive and reconciling work throughout the world.

SCOTT TODD, PHD
Senior Ministry Advisor, Compassion International
Chairman of the Board, AERDO

PREPARING CHURCHES FROM THE MAJORITY WORLD FOR PARTNERSHIP

EDOUARD LESSEGUE, COMPASSION INTERNATIONAL

Edouard Lessegue was born and raised in Port-au-Prince, Haiti, and studied at Bob Jones University in Greenville, South Carolina. In 1993, he was named Haiti's country director for Compassion International. In 2007, Edouard moved with his wife, Gina, and their three children to Deerfield Beach, Florida, where he now serves as the regional vice president of Latin America and the Caribbean region for Compassion International. Compassion International exists as an advocate for children to release them from their spiritual, economic, social, and physical poverty and enable them to become responsible and fulfilled Christian adults. Today, Compassion helps more than 1 million children in 25 different countries.

The church in the Majority World usually is on the receiving end of church-to-church relationships and missionary efforts. As we move closer to authentic partnerships, the church in those parts of the world needs to prepare to play her role in a way that reflects equality in Christ. This is a challenge that we at Compassion International have struggled with for years; in many ways, we still struggle with it. How do we prepare churches in our ministry countries for partnership with a large organization like Compassion? How do we prepare them for partnership with other churches in America, Canada, Australia, and so on?

Because I am a national leader and pastor, this challenge weighs on my mind. As a Haitian church leader, I interact with other national leaders. We wrestle with questions such as: How do we keep our identity and dignity as a national church while engaging in a relationship with a church from the North or with a parachurch organization like Compassion International? I do not bring many answers to these complicated questions, but I hope we can explore together some possible avenues to address the challenge.

Many times we rush through the process of partnership without taking the time to adequately recognize and put in place the necessary building blocks of partnership. We jump into action without developing the foundation of true partnership—solid relationship. This is especially important in cross-cultural (North-South) associations. By not taking the time to build that relationship, we create all kinds of misinterpretations and false expectations that render true partnership almost impossible.

On one hand, lack of relationship causes the church in the South to see our relationship with a parachurch organization or Northern congregation as a funding mechanism and not as true partnership that demonstrates equality in Christ, mutual benefits, and sharing resources and lessons together. Once financial support becomes the primary factor that defines the relationship, the partnership is doomed to fail. On the other hand, lack of relationship causes the church or parachurch organization from the North to want to solve problems for the local church in a paternalistic way, treating that church as a child needing direction, provision, and supervision.

Ernie Addicott in his book, *Body Matters: A Guide to Partnership in Christian Mission* (Interdev Partnership Associates, 2005), provides a number of concepts I will discuss here. The first visible actions in a cross-cultural church relationship are usually the resources exchanged. But rarely is this the true essence of the partnership. Others may say that "common purpose" is the starting point of partnership; however, while it is essential, common purpose is not the foundation of good partnership. True partnership is based on solid relationship.

SHARING RESOURCES

AGREED-UPON PLANS

COMMON PURPOSE

SOLID RELATIONSHIP

Adapted from Ernie Addicott, *Body Matters: A Guide to Partnership in Christian Mission* (Interdev Partnership Associates, 2005).

Building relationship requires time. It takes time for both parties to develop trust, respect, understanding of cultural realities and sensitivities, and communication styles.

As we take time to build relationship, the church must undergo intentional preparation for cross-cultural partnership. This should cover at least three important aspects:

- Theological
- Cultural
- Technical or practical

The church is the bride of Christ, for whom Christ died; the local church is the visible representation of the bride of Christ. This truth carries deep implications for the way the church sees herself and how she relates to others. How many times do we hear or see local church leaders humbly thanking us for partnering with them? I tell them that it is the opposite: We are the ones who should thank them for allowing us to partner with them. Christ died for the church and not for an organization, no matter how powerful and resourceful that organization might be. It is often interesting to note their reaction, as if some light had come on—yes, that is true, the church is important to God.

The church from the Majority World is often referred to as "under-resourced" and so come to view themselves as "lacking." Though these congregations may be under-resourced financially, often they are spiritually rich and vibrant and able to contribute in an authentic two-way relationship.

I recently visited four projects in Nicaragua. Though we did not plan it this way, at least two of the churches had a church-to-church relationship with a congregation in North America. One of these cases stood out—the relationship between a community church in Texas and a Nicaraguan church. Representatives from the Texas church visited the church in Nicaragua on multiple trips, providing well over $15,000 to the Nicaragua church; new classrooms resulted, among other projects. When I asked the Nicaraguan church pastor about his expectations for the partnership, a term he used frequently to describe their relationship with the Texas church, his response was all about what his church would receive and how they would benefit. It did not dawn on him that his congregation could provide blessings to the Texas church as well. When I pressed the notion of mutual benefit in true partnership and that his church did have spiritual gifts the other congregation could benefit from, he thought for a while and shared with me the following story.

During his last visit to Nicaragua, the Texas church pastor, in tears, asked for prayer for his young daughter, who had been diagnosed with cancer. The Nicaraguan church took this to heart, and the church members earnestly prayed and fasted for the pastor's daughter. Three months later, they received word that the pastor's daughter had been healed; the last test did not reveal any trace of cancer. What a beautiful story of sharing each other's burdens in the body of Christ; yet the Nicaraguan church pastor did not see this in the context of mutual benefit of their partnership. Of course, I cannot say God healed the girl because of the Nicaraguans' prayers—I am sure hundreds of people were praying for the girl—but they still participated in the miracle.

Local churches, no matter where they are located, need to recognize and value their spiritual gifts and assets. They need to realize they are capable not only of meeting their own spiritual needs, but also of blessing other "well-resourced" churches. This reminds me of a comment from a church leader in Haiti who mentioned how American churches have the gift of "giving," while Haitian churches have the gift of "receiving." American churches, exercise your gift so our churches may exercise ours! This is such a distorted view of the global church.

In order to effectively play her role in partnership, the church in the South, just like the church in the North, needs to address deeply ingrained cultural values that may stand in the way of true partnership. In the Haitian context, for example, I see at least several cultural mindsets to address in the process of developing any cross-cultural partnership—both at the time of establishing the relationship and throughout the process of relating and working together.

First is the mindset of fatalism, the belief that all events are predetermined by fate and therefore are unalterable—regardless of one's effort or hard work. This concept sounds so foreign to Western thinking, and even to a Christian worldview. But many cultures (and local churches within those cultures) operate with such a mindset. This is prevalent in Haiti.

Second is the mindset of dependency, the belief that people cannot do anything for themselves without a handout or direction from others. The wrong type of relationship between churches reinforces this attitude by communicating that a local church depends on outside help in order to progress. This is obviously counterproductive and harmful to the church.

Third, the church in the developing world needs to understand some of the significant cultural characteristics and values of the Northern culture. These are some of the common cultural differences in cross-cultural (North-South) partnerships.

1. **Accountability.** This is the concept of being responsible to give an account to someone else for one's actions. People in many cultures interpret this as a lack of respect or trust, especially if someone is in a position of leadership or authority. In Compassion, we often face this challenge in our projects. For instance, an auditor dares to ask a project director for documentation of expenses incurred on behalf of the children, and this offends the project director. A pastor does not see the need to answer to a church board or committee. In many cases, it takes years to convince our church partners that accountability is not a sign of weakness or mistrust but a normal part of the partnership—and that actually it can go both ways.

2. **Time.** Northern cultures put a high importance on timeliness, while Southern cultures tend to be more flexible on this notion. For a North American, for instance, a 4 o'clock meeting means that the meeting will start at 4, while for a Haitian typically this means people will start arriving around 4:15 for an opening

prayer at 4:30. In the process of preparation for cross-cultural partnership, the Haitian congregation needs to understand that the North American partner feels offended to have to wait 30 minutes, especially after both sides agreed on a 4:00 meeting time.

3. **Speed.** Speed is another concept cultures value differently. Most Northern cultures hold the underlying belief that doing something faster is inherently better. While these cultures put a priority on accomplishing a task efficiently and quickly, other cultures value relationships generated in the process, often regardless of the time involved.

4. **Integrity.** This is a biblical concept (1 Kings 9:4; Nehemiah 7:2; Job 2:3; Mark 12:14). Integrity speaks of the nature of something that is whole, complete, without blemish. Though Christians from various cultural backgrounds value integrity, they do not necessarily interpret it the same way or emphasize the same aspects. While the Northern Christian sees integrity as a principle to uphold regardless of circumstances, brothers from the South may be a little more lenient. They take into account personal factors, such as efforts and intentions behind an action, before condemning an offender. While recognizing the offense, they may not be as harsh in their judgment. On one hand, this can infuriate Northern Christians and make them look at their brothers as weak and lacking character. On the other hand harsher judgment from the North may frustrate the brothers and sisters from the South and

make them consider their Northern partners legalistic and "heartless."

Obviously such differences may cause a lot of frustration as two partners approach these concepts from their own perspectives and experience. Both partners must clearly explain their values before initiating a partnership and reinforce them throughout the relationship. Partners must unpack the relative significance of these values in order to facilitate cooperation. In all cases, the right biblical understanding must supersede cultural biases and preferences.

Good partnership does not just happen. It takes time, but it also takes training. It requires a cultural shift, but it also requires some practical skills. Those skills are important for any type of partnership, but they are critical in cross-cultural relationships. Otherwise, the small church in the South can be easily overwhelmed by the more sophisticated approach and set of skills of the church from the North. The good news is that these skills can be learned. Skills like decision-making, vision-casting, negotiation, and conflict resolution are essential for good partnership. The church needs to be properly equipped in applying them.

1. **The skill of decision-making.** Ideally, in most partnerships, decisions are made in consensus. However, this is not usually the case for many churches in the Majority World; church leaders are not used to making decisions in consultation with others. Often, the leader's word is final, and leaders prefer that no

the leader's word is final, and leaders prefer that no one question them. They do not make decisions "by committee" or collaboration.

2. **The skill of vision-casting.** Both churches need a strong sense of vision. This is especially important for the churches in the South, since often they are the less sophisticated (in terms of partnership) of the two parties. Helping a congregation formulate a vision for their own church and community must be an intentional investment. It also helps to clarify their expectations for the partnership.

3. **The skill of negotiation.** This is crucial, especially in situations where the church leaders may see themselves as the weaker party. They not only need to know that they can speak up, but how to speak up:

   - How to give and take without losing face
   - How to articulate and defend their priorities without the fear of losing the relationship altogether
   - How to look for a compromise that is acceptable to both

4. **The skill of conflict resolution.** Conflict invariably arises in the course of the partnership, and it is not necessarily sinful. The church needs to know how to draw from the trust and respect the members have for each other in order to adequately solve their differences in a constructive manner.

Cross-cultural partnership takes intentional preparation on both sides. Preparing the church for effective partnership takes time and requires attention on at least three fronts: theological, cultural, and technical.

Summary of Key Points

1. True partnership is based on solid relationship.

2. Cross-cultural partnership should cover at least three important aspects: theological, cultural, and technical or practical.

3. Southern churches may be under-resourced financially, but often they are spiritually rich and vibrant and able to contribute in an authentic two-way relationship.

4. Churches need to recognize their spiritual gifts and assets. They need to realize that they are capable not only of meeting their own spiritual needs, but also of blessing other churches that may be considered more "well-resourced."

5. Good partnership does not just happen. It takes time, but it also takes training. It requires a cultural shift, but it also requires some practical skills.

KINGDOM REVEALED: WE MAKE THE ROAD BY WALKING IT TOGETHER

TOM AND DEE YACCINO, LA RED DEL CAMINO

Tom and Dee Yaccino have partnered in cross-cultural ministry since the late 1980s. Through strategic partnerships developed in the Dominican Republic they participate in and support the development of a church-based network focused on the practice of integral mission called la Red del Camino for Integral Mission in Latin America and the Caribbean (www.lareddelcamino.net) with hundreds of churches in more than nine countries.

Our title, "*We Make the Road by Walking It Together*," is adapted from the classic book of conversations on empowerment, education, and social change between two giants of pedagogy: Paulo Freire and Myles Horton, authors of *We Make the Road by Walking: Conversations on Education and Social Change* (1990). We add the word *together* because we find the redundancy worthwhile. Often, partners "make a road by walking it," but "we" are walking on separate paths. In order to form true partnership, we need to be intentional about walking along the road *together*.

The title also includes the word *road*. We serve and support a network of churches in Latin America called "La Red del Camino" (RDC), which literally means the network "On the *Way*" (or road). The network believes that Jesus is the Way, and we must travel His Way to fully understand it. As we travel along the way together in these church-to-church partnerships, we find it necessary to do a lot of roadwork. What we hope to share here are some of the basic things we learned together along the way as we engage in the process of relational connection between churches from North America and Latin America.

MISSIO DEI

The starting point for church-to-church partnership is discovering what we each believe about *Missio Dei* or God's mission for His world. We must start our journey toward kingdom partnerships here because what we believe about

God's mission will affect what we believe we should be doing as individuals and churches to engage the world. Claudio Oliver, a leader and pastor from an RDC network church in Curitiba, Brazil, says,

> I think that a lot of people actually think that we have a mission, but I think some of the basics in our community of faith is that we don't have a mission, the mission has us. You know, this is different, because the mission is bigger than our thing, our community, or our life. The mission is a mystery. The mystery is to put together what has been broken by sin, or has been separated, and to suture all these things together again and heal it. The Lord so loved the cosmos, that He sent His son for anyone who decided to believe in Him to take part in this cosmic salvation (or suturing) that is performed by the Lord. This is His plan. It's not about me. It's about the world…and I take part of this mission of God as part of the world.

We talk about *Missio Dei* because we really feel that in partnership, part of God's overarching plan for the restoration of all things is that we come together in Christ as brothers and sisters at our Father's table, realizing the good news; we are all significant players in His mission as citizens of the kingdom of God. When we come together, we discover what each brings to the table to contribute to His divine plan. This may seem like a simplistic understanding of the gospel, yet we often see churches coming into cross-cultural partnership with the understanding that "we" have a mission as church "x." So, we (from here) are going to go and do our mission (there), but we want them to do it together with us. Can you see how this creates a dilemma from the start?

A FALSE FRAMEWORK

This distorted way of thinking tends to separate us from one another rather than bring us together. It tends to create competition, territorialism, and conflict rather than foster community, reconciliation, and restoration. This way of thinking has been ingrained in all of us from the time of Adam's sin. It sets up a worldly logic that informs us that our worth or worthiness (our identity or "name") comes as a result of the fruit of our labor instead of the unmerited grace and favor of our Creator. So we set out to prove our worth—even as Christians, and even when most of us confess that we have been saved by grace, not by any merit of our own (see Ephesians 2:8-9). We unwittingly continue to operate within the same worldly framework from which we were saved.

We must think about this framework as we seek partnership because we experience its effects on us all along the way. We start out on the road with such good intentions to come together in global Christian partner relationships and end up lying beaten, half-naked in a ditch somewhere out in the middle of nowhere. What is going on? Why does it seem harder to develop authentic global partner relationships than we think it should be?

We are all born into a framework, a system, or a logic that informs us and conditions us to do everything we do—even global "mission." But that framework is a false framework that was established at the fall of humankind by the prince of this world in an attempt to undermine God's design for His creation. The false framework seduces us all into believing the lie that we must prove we have a name or purpose above and beyond others. Believing the lie pits us against God and others in competition instead of putting us in community with God and others in the favor and *shalom* God intended for us in creation.

This way of thinking bleeds into every other activity in our lives, including the way we go about relating with one another in global church-to-church partnership. So we must reframe everything. In the RDC network, we call it a form of detoxification. It means intentionally dismantling a structure of logic governing our human relations since Adam with the original sin that is at the heart of all sources of domination, social-class disparity, spirit of conquest, and expansionism. We need to be aware we inherited this Adamic logic by default. Unwittingly we use it to legitimize the will of the powerful by presenting them as benefactors over those in need.

When we use language like *benefactors* and *beneficiaries*, often inadvertently we speak from within the framework of the world. We go about partnership as we do everything else, and all of us are enslaved and imprisoned to it and blinded by the world's framework. But Jesus warns us against the world's logic. In Luke 22, after having walked for three years up close and personal with Jesus, the disciples got into an argument over position and who was considered the greatest—who had the name that drew crowds, if you will (Luke 22:24). The conflict stemmed from the worldly framework that conditioned them to think in terms of power as the solution for the oppression and powerlessness they had lived with all their lives. They were thinking of Jesus' kingdom in terms of worldly kingdoms with a distinct line of hierarchy, authority, and power. They truly believed that as they entered Jerusalem, they would be assigned earthly positions of power and authority in the kingdom of God that Jesus was always talking about. With that power and authority they would *now* really be able to do some good in the world. And what does Jesus say? "The kings of the Gentiles lord it over them; and those who exercise authority over them call themselves Benefactors. But you are not to be like that. Instead, the greatest among you should be like the youngest, and the one who rules like the one who serves" (Luke 22:25-26).

Why the stern warning from Jesus? What is so wrong with being a benefactor? Does it relate to how we relate church-to-church around the globe? Do churches with resources and big names and worldly "success" come to other churches in relationship as benefactors—as if they had the right by the power vested in them and because of their relative position of authority to make whatever they want happen? What is the potential danger inherent in that thinking?

KINGDOM-OF-GOD FRAMEWORK

When Jesus said, "Don't lord it over them" to His disciples, He juxtaposed their "kingdom of this world" framework with His "kingdom of God" framework to help them see their false rationalization. Jesus said, "My kingdom is not of this world" (John 18:36). God's kingdom is not based on the fruit of our labor; it is not based on what we deserve or do not deserve because of what we possess or do not possess. It is not based on our name, or our church's name, or our mission's name. The kingdom of God is meant to be attractive, distinct from the kingdom of this world and based on the unmerited favor and grace bestowed on us as the creation of God. We are supposed to operate as kingdom citizens in ways that distinguish us from the worldly counterfeit. Jesus fully expects us to go about kingdom business as if what He said were true. The problem is that even as His followers, we fall back into the conditioning and programming we received when we were born into this world—not the new creative, transformative, innovative reprogramming we receive as we are *born again* through Christ into a new created order called the kingdom of God.

When we are aware of the fact that we often tend to move back into our worldly framework of thinking as we go about doing mission, partnership, development, and transformational community work, we see how it affects all patterns of response in relating with one another. It affects our understanding of power, our understanding of wealth, of relationships, of poverty, of the results we seek to achieve together, and even our understanding of what success will look like.

CONTRASTING OUR PARTNERSHIP ACTIONS BETWEEN THE TWO FRAMEWORKS

As we look at global partnerships, we want to show how this plays out by comparing and contrasting three areas affected by our frameworks: the relationships, the resources, and the results. We want to break it down into what it looks like from both perspectives (in our case, North American and Latin American partner churches). First, we will see the tendencies and patterns at work when both operate from a kingdom-of-this-world framework and then what it might look like as we consider operating in terms of the kingdom-of-God framework.

We compare two perspectives from within the one larger framework of the kingdom of this world. One side is the context of the "West," which we call the "Minority West" (also referred to in various settings as the *North, resourced, developed, sending, supporting,* etc.). The other side is the context of the "Majority Rest" (also referred to in various setting as the *South, under-resourced, developing, two-thirds, receiving, implementing,* etc.) Each operates within the worldly framework to justify by the fruit of one's labor or to make a name for oneself, but with a bit of a different angle.

Relationships

Relationships in the Minority West often are agenda-driven. We see the relational transaction as a business deal. We seek a name for ourselves in terms of our mission, what we are going do, and what we've accomplished. We assume that our partner needs or even wants our help—whatever that may look like. When we send short-term teams to do "mission," we focus on our spiritual transformation. We use short-term teams as a means to grow our people and really don't look at what the implications are for the others on the other end. Individuals and churches get a type of short-term mission ADHD (attention deficit hyperactivity disorder). We go from one experience to another and may think, "Okay, I've done that, I've done that, went to Dominican Republic, okay, gotta go to Uganda next, okay, over here next." People develop a mentality of "been there, done that, what's next?" The duration of the relationship is pragmatic, usually dependent on the length of the project or program.

From the Majority Rest perspective, we accept the belief, based on the history of colonization, that "we are going to have to jump through some hoops to be able to get what we really need." We will take advantage of the relationship for the benefits that we need. Needs for resources, technology, and so on are legitimate, but we expect to do whatever the "owner" or "donor" of that resource or technology wants. That's the only way to gain that advantage or benefit. Sometimes churches and individuals seek identity through making ties and associations with a larger partner church from the North by becoming representatives of their mission, movement, or church. We will tolerate paternalism because we are already used to it. We have a long history with it in order to achieve our goals. We accommodate teams, sometimes at the cost of our own ministries, if there is an agenda-driven framework from the West saying, "We just need to get our people out there to get their hands dirty." We will accommodate and do something so their hands can get dirty, but whether or not the effort adds value to anything we do is questionable. The perspective of the Majority Rest is that relationship equals opportunity.

In the kingdom-of-God framework, on the other hand, both partners learn that the *relationship is the end*; it is not the means to an end. And that end is oneness. Jesus' prayer in John 17 is that God is glorified and His kingdom is revealed when we truly are one as children of the same Father. From this framework, we share an understanding of the mission of God, our role in it, and that it takes time. We are on a journey together in community to work things out, even to begin to figure out what we are going to do together, and the timeline is eternal. Obviously, we face specific timeframes as we enter into initiatives we plan together, but even as the relationship morphs as we walk together, we do not abandon the established friendship. Just as a marriage partnership is expected to last "until death do us part," being partners in global relations requires a commitment for the long haul. Our friend in the Brazilian RDC network paraphrases a quote from C.S. Lewis by saying, "If something is not important for eternity, it is eternally unimportant." In the RDC network the motto is, "If we're not friends, we can't work together. We have to be friends first."

Resources

In another important aspect of church-to-church part-nerships, resources, the Minority West (within the worldly framework) tends to pour resources onto the campfires lit to eradicate global poverty around the world. We tend to see a lack of economic resources as the root of the problem of poverty. Our solution is to keep this or that project or program going so we can give our partners a share of the economic wealth with which we are blessed, or to set up services that will provide basic needs for others. And we do it because we can. We have enough money, enough people power, enough belief in what we are doing to keep something going forever— even if it's not really working. If the solution were resources alone, the billions of dollars spent over the last 50 years or so in "development theory" history would have resulted in lasting change. Yet we insist our money will solve the problem. We exhibit our sense of entitlement to make the rules, manage the risk, and protect our interests and investments because we gave others our resources to help make it possible.

On the other hand, the Majority Rest learned to fan those flames so that the logs burn up so that we can get more logs. We, too, believe in the power of resources to change our circumstances and know how to fan the flames to keep the flow. The Minority Rest shows the same sense of entitlement in a different way. It is expressed as an attitude: "You owe me." So we are willing to follow the rules, secure those funds, play the victim or beneficiary role. Project ADHD strikes this side.

We think, "Okay, there's money in wells, let's go do wells. Or there's money for AIDS, we should do AIDS. Now there's money for such and such . . . " We jump from one project or program to the next to ensure some kind of economic benefit or provision for a real or felt need. Obviously, this kind of thinking about resources from the kingdom-of-this-world framework creates dependency. It also may create a kind of elitism among churches in the context of those receiving the resources. The church that receives the blessing gains status for being able to secure the much coveted resources and may begin to monopolize its hold on them to maintain its good standing instead of sharing the wealth.

In the kingdom-of-God framework, we all share at our Father's table. The resources are God's resources, not ours to hoard or ours to control. "My resources" or "your resources" shifts to "we are all resources." Everything we possess and all of who we are is an opportunity to bless somebody else. We are around a big banquet table with our Heavenly Father, and He is the one who redistributes the elements and says, "I think that needs to go there and this needs to go here." We are all an important part of making that happen and blessing each other as fellow partakers at the table. We are God's primary resource, and therefore when we are in relationship, God reveals to us things we didn't even know we could contribute to His work of redemption. That is the beauty of the relational aspect.

Another important kingdom-of-God perspective is that the blessing continues to bless others in a multiplier effect. It is what the RDC leaders call the "5 & 2 Principle." When Jesus saw the hungry multitude, He asked His disciples to do something. But their conditioned response was very much in line with the kingdom-of-this-world framework: "Eight months' wages would not buy enough bread for each one to have a bite!" (John 6:7). "Send the crowds away, so they can go to the villages and buy themselves some food" (Mathew 14:15). But Jesus reframes the situation when He commands, "Bring [the loaves and the bread] here to me" (Matthew 14:18). The "5 & 2 Principle" is giving what we have, what we know, and our experiences to Jesus so He will do the miracle. But it takes that step of faith to give our resources over to Him. The miracle was not necessarily that the fish and bread multiplied; the miracle was that they *gave up* five loaves and two fish (which would not be enough to feed Peter) and let Jesus do His thing with them.

The same principle applies to global partner relationships. We must all give up our control over what we think we have and allow Jesus to take it in order to cause an unexpected exponential multiplier effect. In partnership, it is important to identify others who share this passion to come together and see what God will do. We look for people who are already doing something with their five loaves and two fish. And we often don't start anything with people who are not using what they've already got.

Results

The third major aspect of church-to-church global partnership is how we define results in both contexts from within the kingdom-of-this-world framework. For the Minority West we need measurable, quantifiable results—bigger is better.

"Scalability" for growth is a given in project planning. The more people the better, the more kids in the program the better, even if it means overstepping the capacity of the local church. We know the program can take only 200 kids, but we need 300. Try anyway! After all, we have the resources, so let's do it. We also like to control the outcomes. We like quick fixes (if we can get a measurable result in 12 months, that is best), because if we show fast results, we'll get more money to do more things, to do bigger things that are scalable. Scalability is a term that we get from the business world (which, by the way, is also part of the kingdom-of-this-world framework). Jesus never talked about scalability. He talked about mustard seeds and leaven.

On the other hand, the Majority Rest from within the kingdom of this world are going to see themselves as insignificant for what they offer. If we are not big enough, then obviously we are not good enough. This thinking ties back to the whole making-a-name concept. We feel pressured to produce, even when it does not make sense for our context. Sometimes even when it is difficult to achieve within limited timeframes, others expect to see a return on their investments. We spin our wheels, hoping that if we can create enough smoke, we will at least get the attention of those with resources.

Results in the kingdom-of-God framework are defined differently—some would even say upside down. Jesus said we might not even be able to see it (probably because we are not looking for it in the right place). He said that it was going to happen, but that the Spirit was the One in control. He compared it to small things like a mustard seed. The mustard seed is a weed that spreads without any control. The people listening to that parable understood that and probably thought it strange that Jesus would compare the kingdom of God to a mustard seed. People did not usually want mustard seeds in their gardens because they were unpredictable and uncontrollable. When we engage in relationships to have partnerships for God's redemptive plans, the outcomes continually will amaze us. We will not necessarily be able to map them out. We can't always say that in a five-year period this is what things are going to look like. There is freedom in that, but there is no safety net for those who need one. In the kingdom of God, size does not matter. Some incredibly small things we may barely be able to see with our worldly eyes are cause for amazing heavenly celebration.

Likewise, the journey is the destination. The process of getting to wherever we are going together matters, and if something great happens because we are walking together, the journey has added value. In our work with RDC, we use a little equation:

$$2 + the\ ONE = \infty$$

When two or more are gathered in His name, plus one (the One), it equals infinity. God is able to open an infinite number of possibilities as we get together in His name.

As we come together to connect as global partners, we constantly must go back and check from within which framework we are operating. We all feel the pressure of the kingdom-of-this-world framework that has conditioned and programmed us to perform in ways that actually are quite contrary to the kingdom of God that we say we believe in. The pressure we feel to produce, or the despair we feel when we fail to produce the results we want, or the shame we sense when we do not make the name for ourselves that we desire, sucks the joy out of the honor and privilege God gives us to serve Him and His kingdom and be a part of His redemptive plans.

AN ILLUSTRATION

A story wraps this all together. A North American church came into a church-to-church partner relationship with a church from Latin America with an obvious kingdom-of-this-world paradigm. The North American leaders made a vision discovery trip. At first they were saying things like, "Okay, we have all these resources. We had the fund drive. We raised lots of money, and now we want to do something. We want to get involved; what are we going to do?"

This was the first time this North American church had visited a group of pastors from churches in the RDC network. It was just an investigatory visit to see where the affinity might lie. But suddenly it turned into a question of "What are we going to do?" "How can we engage these people?" "How can we invest resources?" We in RDC, as bridge people, recognized partnership does not happen all at once even after we under-stand the way our framework affects us. We said something like, "Let's take some time for you to really get to know each other before we start talking about those things." So we spent more time eating around tables and listening to each other's stories and understanding we were all present as a part of God's redemptive plan —whatever, wherever, and with whomever that may be.

But it was so frustrating for the North American church. The whole time they were sitting on their hands just like kids who wanted to get their hands in the cookie jar. And we were not sure if this was going to work well. The worldly framework was at play, convincing them that time is money. They expected to be treated a certain way because, "Hey, we're professionals with tons of experience and knowledge to offer." We so often come to the relationship in terms of what we know, what we have, our position. It is so much easier to live by kingdom-of-this-world principles than to follow the kingdom-of-God principles because the world doesn't ask you to die to yourself.

Then, five years later (this church has been in process now for five years), the partners understand the relational foundation of partnership that comes before results. Synergistic opportunities took place in both contexts because these churches from diverse realities with unique contributions to God's mission took the time to get to know one another so that they know what is important to do together. If they had not taken that time, none of the things they do now would be remotely within the realm of possibility in their heads— certainly not during those first few meetings in the first year.

We see this serendipitous mutual kingdom business going on because these churches had the courage to trade the lie for the truth and trust that operating from within God's framework would bring them together and take them farther than they could operating from within a worldly framework. On the journey, each learned to live as attractive, alternative examples of what true global partnership can be like in the kingdom of God. The challenge is to show others that even though things may go wrong (and, believe us, when they go wrong, they can go horribly wrong), even though some may be convinced we would all be better off if everyone would just stay out of every-body else's way all together, we are persuaded that connecting through global partner relationships is worth every effort to do well. When they go well, when churches come together as diverse, autonomous, global citizens of the kingdom of God in humility, respect, mutuality, integrity, and community, abso-lutely nothing compares to the distinct, mysterious beauty of oneness the world sees in the bridal gown of Christ knit together church by church by church by church.

Summary of Key Points

1. The starting point for church-to-church partnership is discovering what we each believe about *Missio Dei* or God's mission for His world. We must start our journey toward kingdom partnerships here because what we believe about God's mission will affect what we believe we should be doing as individuals and churches to engage in the world.

2. In the kingdom-of-God framework, on the other hand, both partners learn that the *relationship is the end*; it is not the means to an end. And that end is oneness.

3. A kingdom-of-God view of resources is that together we are God's primary resource. Therefore when we are in relationship, God reveals to us things we didn't even know we could contribute to His work of redemption. That is the beauty of the relational aspect.

4. We must all give up our control over what we think we possess and allow Jesus to take it in order to cause an unexpected exponential multiplier effect. In partnership, it is important to identify others with this passion to come together and see what God will do.

5. When we engage in relationships of partnerships for God's redemptive plans, the outcomes continually will amaze us. We will not necessarily be able to map them out and say that in a five-year period this is what things are going to look like. There is freedom in that, but there is no safety net for those who need it. In the kingdom of God, size does not matter.

POWER DIFFERENTIALS IN PARTNERSHIPS: A CONFESSION AND CALL

STEPHAN BAUMAN, WORLD RELIEF

Stephan Bauman is the senior vice president of programs for World Relief, where he leads approximately 2,500 staff in 20 nations. Stephan oversees programs in the health, economic, agriculture, and refugee areas. Stephan joined World Relief in 2005 as the country director in Rwanda. Prior to this, Stephan served as director of international programs for World Hope International, where he oversaw relief and development programs in 25 countries worldwide in the agriculture, education, economic development, anti-trafficking, and health sectors.

I repent!

In 1999 my wife and I lived on a hospital ship in West Africa near Sierra Leone, where rebels waged a horrific war. Rebel armies conscripted young boys and forced them to terrorize mothers, fathers, and siblings with AK47s and machetes. We helped our friends, Moses and Sally, to evacuate the country. After weeks of difficult communication and careful planning, Moses and Sally escaped from rebel-held Freetown and made their way to the Guinea border. On the way, they witnessed the execution of an innocent girl. I'll never forget the moment they arrived at our ship. Sally collapsed to the floor and convulsed in tears. She thanked God for safe ground.

In the weeks and months that followed, first on the ship and later at a debriefing center near Geneva, our friendship with Moses and Sally grew. Those who suffer together grow together. We shared life. We sang. We laughed. During that time, I asked Moses to tell me how he felt about Americans, about the West, particularly about those seeking to "help Africa." His first response struck me: he told me I didn't want to know. Some days later I asked him again. He agreed to talk after I promised him it would not affect our friendship.

What I heard next changed my life.

He told me *I* had the power; he did not. We speak, they listen. We give, Africans receive. He said they are not allowed to question. They must accept because they *must*, even if they know an effort will fail. They smile, they bless, they honor. And he told me how they hurt when we leave because they never hear from us again.

It took me seven years in Africa to develop a deep enough friendship for an African to tell me the truth. Moses spoke; I listened as he plunged a knife into my heart.

I repented that day and, from time to time, I repent still.

SHEDDING POWER AND JOINING THE POWERLESS

Cultural change generally occurs in this way: an important person or event triggers a movement that starts from the center and flows to the margins. Political movements gain momentum in capital cities. Entertainers influence from Hollywood. Fashion trends begin in Paris or Milan. Financiers on Wall Street, London, or Hyderabad launch new business ventures. Cultural change follows the flow of power.

But Jesus was different. Israel was unknown to the Roman world, and Galilee was the backwater of Hebrew life. Along with Jesus, 12 uneducated, blue-collar men—less the educated one, Judas—changed the course of history. The movement of Jesus *began* at the margins. And it's continually renewed at the margins to this day. Remember David, the shepherd boy who became king? Mary, the young peasant? Or how about your least likely friend who now leads a powerful ministry? The move of God is from the powerless to the powerful, from the margins to the middle.

Joke van Opstal is World Relief's least likely. Born in Holland, she was rejected in her youth by family and friends. She studied nursing and found herself in the midst of a Christian youth movement in her teens. Joke moved to Cambodia and helped birth a Cambodian-led ministry called *The Way of Hope*. This movement of 6,000 Christ followers, organized into more than 800 cell churches, reaches out to children and families in more than 162 villages in 5 provinces. More than 37,000 children are involved in the associated community health program, and more than 5,000 volunteers are active in raising HIV/AIDS awareness, providing education and home visiting.

Rowan Williams, archbishop of Canterbury, speaks eloquently to this theme:

> Attempts to bypass local networks, local styles of decision-making and above all local rationales for action or change invariably produce resentment and puzzlement. What people see is an agenda that is not theirs, activated by foreigners claiming to act on their behalf. . . . If development processes and programs are not to be paralyzed by such resentment and mistrust, with the result that local communities cannot see themselves as agents of their own change, enormous potential is left unrealized.[1]

When my friend Moses spoke truth to me, God asked me to begin a new journey—a journey that would require me to shed the position of power and take up the posture of humility. Sure, my intentions were good. I sought the best for my brothers and sisters in Africa. But my best intentions were hurtful.[2] Deep inside, unconsciously perhaps, I believed my "prosperity," skills, and knowledge qualified me to bring "good news" to Africa. I subtly identified myself as the "benefactor" and my fellow Africans as the "beneficiaries." I lived out a power differential that was hurtful.

God sees things differently. All have fallen short. All are broken. All are poor. He became poor so we could become rich.[3] And He asks us to follow Him.

We must shed our power and join the powerless. *But how?* We must begin by recognizing the superiority we convey— intentionally or not. We must repent. Then we must find practical ways, even simple ways, to demonstrate humility. We can express our need to those we serve and show our great dependence on Christ as our source, our only source. We can ask those we seek to serve instead to give to us. Have them pray for us. Ask for advice. Become a child again and learn their language. Carry friendships beyond the visit, the task, the project. Honor them as they honor us. Listen, listen, and then listen again.[4]

CHURCH DOING AND CHURCH BEING

The worldwide church is the largest institution in the world. It has enormous potential to effect change. For many of us, the church is the primary vehicle for reaching out to the world's vulnerable.

But is the church just a vehicle for change, or is it something more? We lived in Rwanda during 2005 and 2006 and worked with thousands of local churches across nearly 100 denominations. I saw the best and worst of local churches. In one particular meeting, I asked a group of Rwandan pastors about their programs and our partnership. They cited examples of lay members serving people living with AIDS. They told of orphaned children now back in school. They spoke of how their congregations welcomed people living with HIV among them.

But they also told me they "felt used" by World Relief and that our agenda was "too narrow." We don't just "do church, we live church," they said.

Our Lord calls His church to *do*. But He also calls His church to *be*. Our tendency, especially when working in the Majority World, is to view the church as a means to end, as a vehicle to serve the oppressed. But some[5] agree with my Rwandan friends, saying the church herself is not only a *vehicle* for mission, but also the *goal* of mission, "in constant need of repentance and conversion" to become all it's meant to be as the bride of Christ.[6]

The *Way of Hope* movement in Cambodia is both a *vehicle of mission* reaching out to the greater community and also an *object of mission* for renewal, discipleship, and, most important, worship. The cells are little communities of hope fully incarnated within the pressing problems of the rural Cambodian landscape. The cells define and redefine their outreach mandate according to emerging issues. They are able to outlive their initial outreach task, adapting to the changing needs of the community, because they exist *to be*, not only *to do*.

We must stop misusing the church. But how? Most important, we must de-emphasize our agenda and emphasize the journey.[7] If we do not properly and carefully place goals and tasks within the context of long-term relationship, our ministry is perceived as transactional. Transactional ministry implies a contract: the parties agree to deliverables, pay money, set expectations, and, as a result, quickly cast identities. Someone plays the role of benefactor; the other plays the role of beneficiary. As a result, the feeling of entitlement settles in on both sides.

Strong relationships—where people in relationship address power differentials through humility, listening, and honesty—provide a foundation for *transformational* ministry. Partners place agendas in their proper context. Relationship and mutual change continue beyond the life of the task, project, or program. Rather than entitlement, *co-creation*, the joy of building something together in friendship, characterizes the relationship.

Of course transformational ministry is more difficult than the transactional ministry. Transformation takes time. Rarely is anything of worth built in a hurry. We must slow down else our good intentions hurt.

FROM HELPING THE POOR TO LETTING THE POOR HELP

"What can you do that an African cannot?" These words from an African friend still echo in my head like a tin bucket falling down cellar stairs. Too often, though well intended, we seek to work "for the poor"[8] or even "with the poor." In so doing, we stifle local initiative.[9] Such posture and corresponding models of ministry can further entrench poverty, especially the forms of poverty that result when our friends already feel inferior.[10] Ministry "by the poor" within their own communities has the potential to transform from the inside out. Ownership is higher. Change lasts and even multiplies.

Cambodia's *Way of Hope* allows those marginalized and on the periphery to become actors in solving their own community problems, representing empowerment in its truest form. *Way of Hope* is known as a "church without walls," meeting primarily beneath homes built on stilts. Cells consist of 8 to 15 people and multiply before they get to 16.[11] They choose which community issues they want to work on. They reach out, engage their neighbors, and multiply to include them. Those they help quickly become helpers themselves.

The savings club movement is another example. Rural moms, dads, even kids come together on a weekly or bimonthly basis to place a bit of savings into a community fund. Members can borrow from this fund and pay a small amount of interest that is later divided among the members. School fees are paid, kids eat more nutritious food, and moms can start small businesses. And who did it? They did it. They helped each other.

Seeking ways to allow the poor to become helpers or actors in their own community change represents the difference between a program and a movement. Programs aren't necessarily bad. In fact, many are helpful if they are designed well and done in the context of long-term relationship. But they can lean towards begin transactional. Movements are transformational, with the potential to carry on as a collective journey.

I began with a confession. Allow me to end with a call. Would you join me in delving deeper into these issues? Repent if you need to. Repent on behalf of others, on behalf of Americans, on behalf of the West.[12] Take on the posture of poverty in tangible ways. Put yourself into positions of need before our friends in Africa, Asia, or Latin America. Be courageous. Take the time to develop long-term relationships with our partners in the Global South. And, most of all, listen.

And then listen again.

Summary of Key Points

1. We need to repent of attitudes of superiority and paternalism.

2. The move of God generally is from the powerless to the powerful, from the margins to the middle.

3. We must shed our power and join the powerless by finding practical ways to demonstrate humility. Have them pray for us. Ask for advice. Learn their language. Carry friendships beyond the visit, the task, the project. Honor them as they honor us and, most important, listen.

4. The church herself is not only a *vehicle* for mission, but also the *goal* of mission, "in constant need of repentance

and conversion" to become all it's meant to be as the bride of Christ.

5. We must de-emphasize our agenda and emphasize the journey. Strong relationships—where people in relationship address power differentials through humility, listening, and honesty—provide a foundation for *transformational* ministry.

EXCELLENCE IN CROSS-CULTURAL PARTNERSHIPS: POVERTY AND THE MISSION OF GOD

JOEL EDWARDS, MICAH CHALLENGE INTERNATIONAL

Rev. Joel Edwards is the international director for Micah Challenge. Joel has a long history with the campaign since its inception in 2000. He was part of the team that created the Challenge campaign partnership between Micah Network and the World Evangelical Alliance and was instrumental in forming the Micah Call. Joel was also co-chair of Micah Challenge from 2004–2007. Prior to his role within Micah Challenge, Joel was general director of the Evangelical Alliance U.K., a post he held for more than 11 years. Joel is committed to harmonize matters of faith, justice, and equality in the public square and to advocate on behalf of the world's poor.

I have a personal as much as a professional interest in the whole idea of cross-cultural missions. People often ask me where I'm from. My usual response is, "I'm from Africa, but I left there about 300 years ago and stopped off in Jamaica for 8 years. Then I spent the rest of my life in the U.K." It's been an interesting journey because, for me, each day is something of a culture shock. Learning to become culturally bilingual is a part of the way God led me over the years in my own ministry, having the pleasure of working as the general director of the Evangelical Alliance in the U.K. I am the first black appointment in a predominantly white evangelical outfit. Cross-cultural work is central to me and even more so in my involvement with Micah Challenge since its inception and now as its international director.

Cross-cultural partnership is vital to all we do. The Micah Network mandates it because the organization represents 300 relief and developmental organizations, and the World Evangelical Alliance mandates it because that organization represents some 420 million people. This cross-fertilizing of constituencies compels us to partnership on their behalf and together with them to advocate for the Millennium Development Goals. These goals are 8 historic commitments that 189 nations made in 2000 to cut extreme poverty in half by 2015.

This means that Micah Network is very much at the cross-roads of different cultural experiences in a critical ministry at a critical time. And when working with some 40 different national campaigns, the discussion of collaboration and partnership becomes central. One of the things I find in this business of cross-cultural partnership is the issue of empowerment—particularly from the North to the South. People I work with predominantly in the South still find is difficult to hear me say, "In order for me to serve to you, you must lead me, even though I'm called international director." People who have come to our conferences in the Global North and whom we bring as spokespersons to significant events experience this reality. Still these people find it hard to hear me ask them for leadership. One of the most desperate needs we have in cracking this stubborn nut is to know how to penetrate the attitudes, values, and self-perception of Southern leaders who find it difficult to think of themselves as leaders when in the company of Northern representatives.

As the international director of Micah Challenge, indigenizing advocacy in the heart of the church particularly challenges me. I describe myself as a church leader at large, and as such I find it challenging to explore ways that partnership with the church and through the church actually takes hold. I'm trying to think my way through precisely what we mean by *mission* in the context of partnership and advocacy.

RECLAIMING THE MEANING OF MISSION

Mission has morphed over the last 30 years—and that can only be a good thing. Increasingly most of us recognize there's a lot more to missions than sending people somewhere else to talk about Jesus with people who have never heard about Him.

That was certainly the view I grew up with. If you were going to be a missionary, some agency would send you to a far-flung region against your better judgment.

Increasingly we recognize that the notion of mission is far more immediate than that. Today new insights about God's mission in the world overwhelm us. Consequently, mission in the 21st century has been reloaded. As the Anabaptist Stuart Murray puts it, "Mission is not an agenda item—it is the agenda. . . . Mission not the church is the starting point."[1]

All of this has important implications for our cross-cultural partnerships against injustices. For our purposes, I want to point to four of these.

1. The Mission of the Church is Global in Nature.

This new response to missions in effect redefined not just the church's *activity* in the world but the church itself. In our cross-cultural work, the global nature of the church is not of key importance. The global nature of the *mission* of the church is important. I contend that this was true from the very foundations of the Christian community. Within the multicultural setting of the early church, maligned Christians became attractive as a result of great miraculous deeds, but even more so as a result of their indiscriminate kindness.[2] Our recovered memory of the priority of missions over ecclesiology is the most fundamental drive giving biblical legitimacy to the new relationship between Christian nongovernmental organizations and the local church. This, more than strategic benefit or long-term survival, must be the basis of our appeal for closer relationships with the local church.

2. God's Love Is Multidimensional.

Second, our recovery of missions shows us the multidimensional nature of God's love for people. Our fear of a social gospel, which sprang up in the 1930s to weaken the power of the Cross, blinded us to the comprehensive nature of God's mission in the world. But as Vinay Samuel reminds us, the object of missions is to "enable God's vision of society to be actualized in all relationships, social, economic, and spiritual."[3] The resurgence of integral missions as expressed through global networks such as Micah Network is a clear expression of this.

This was indeed the great unveiling at the Lausanne Conference in 1974. We affirm God as both the Creator and the Judge of all people. We therefore should share His concern for justice and reconciliation throughout human society and for the liberation of men and women from every kind of oppression. Because men and women are made in the image of God, every person, regardless of race, religion, color, culture, class, sex, or age, has an intrinsic dignity. On this basis, he or she should be respected and served, not exploited. Here too we express penitence both for our neglect and for having sometimes regarded evangelism and social concern as mutually exclusive. Reconciliation with other people is not reconciliation with God. Social action is not evangelism. Political liberation is not salvation. Nevertheless we affirm that evangelism and socio-political involvement are both part of our Christian duty (Acts 17:26, 31; Genesis 18:25; Isaiah 1:17; Psalm 45:7; Genesis 1:26-27; James 3:9; Leviticus 19:18; Luke 6:27, 35; James 2:14-26; John 3:3, 5; Matthew 5:20; Matthew 6:33; 2 Corinthians 3:18; James 2:20).[4]

Lausanne was groundbreaking. As we approach Lausanne 2010 I hope the church will build on this biblical imperative, because cross-cultural partnership demands it. It would be a travesty for missions if Lausanne 2010 did not embrace and amplify its voice against injustice precisely at a time when the world will be shouting out loud on this issue.

3. The Gospel Is Cross-Cultural.

Third, missions is fundamentally cross-cultural not because it is culturally fluid and contextual—important though that is—but because the gospel is cross-cultural.[5] What Dr J. I. Packer once described as God's "cosmic generosity" is the fountainhead of our global appeal. Mission is inconceivable apart from the idea that the God who is everybody's God sent Jesus to die for everyone so that everyone may have life in all its fullness.[6]

4. Missions Goes Beyond the Church.

Fourth, missions happens beyond the church and often begins within the fabric of society.

The church is arrogant to suppose we bring God's mission to an unsuspecting and uninterested world. Missions invariably is God's response to the pain of a world that, as Paul would tell us, groans in expectation of a response from us.[7]

Our task is to enable people to see that missions is a dance between the call of our culture and God's ability to respond through His church. The world does not initiate missions. Rather, God awakens a need to which the church is primed to respond and in which she participates in order to make God known. "The vision and work of the Spirit," says Michael Riddell, "is broader than the imaginations of the faithful."[8]

The Reformation, for example, is inconceivable without the great explosion of culture and classical languages that preceded it. We call this the Renaissance. With all its intellectual challenges, some evangelicals saw the Age of Reason as a new dawn. Protestantism and evangelicalism were both child and midwife of our modern age.[9] The great missionary movement of the 18th and 19th centuries was so closely associated with the age of imperial expansionism that we exploited the same people in Africa, Asia, and the Americas whom we evangelized. William Carey's "Expect great things, achieve great things" slogan was itself a by-product of Enlightenment entrepreneurialism.[10] David Bosch's reminder that 19th century missions was a "child of the modern mind" is a sobering reminder of how missions tends to begin in our world.

And of course we can say the same for the movement

to end slavery that took place against the backdrop of revolutions across Europe and a growing passion for individual freedoms and civil liberties. The movement for the abolition of slavery was so identified with the revolutions across Europe that William Wilberforce, the great abolitionist, was accused of being a revolutionary.

None of this displaces the work of the Spirit in the life of the church. It is merely an honest contextualization that we are prone to edit from our rhetoric and message. But I believe it's very important.

GOD'S MISSION TO THE POOR

We may attempt to involve the church in the work of integral missions by spending many millions to motivate the body of Christ to become involved in missions to the poor. And in this effort, Christ followers should hear a clear message: we should get involved in poverty reduction because the Bible says so. But they should also hear that this is what the Spirit is saying now to the church about the world.

So what if this is what the Spirit already said in the world? And what if this mission to the poor is God's way of making Himself intelligible to the world?

This is not to say that the church was not involved with missions to the poor in the past. Any study will show that historically the church was at the helm of social care and alleviating poverty. But none of us can doubt that our world has risen up during recent times in an unprecedented way to speak out against injustice and environmental concerns. God's mission in the world may co-opt a plethora of organizations such as Live Aid, Africa Aid, the United Nations Millennium Development Goals, and Global Call to Action Against Poverty. Bono, Sting, and Geldof are uncharacteristic prophets!

In this context, our involvement in God's mission to the poor is both urgent and consistent with the Bible. Care of the poor is pure and faultless religion[11] and entirely in harmony with people whose good works shine before men who then glorify the Father.[12] And surely it was more than a coincidence that when the church took time to address the issue of injustice in her care of widows, not only did she experience accelerated growth, but she also won over society's skeptical professionals.[13]

Robinson and Smith are right to remind us that Wesley's revival was not immediately responsible for the growth of the British church in the 18th and 19th centuries. Thirty-five years after Wesley's revival, evangelical Christians still stood ridiculed on the margins of society. If Martin Robinson and Dwight Smith are right, churches began to grow in the aftermath of the church's involvement in the abolitionist movement. "No one became engaged in a campaign to abolish slavery in order to boost church attendance, yet paradoxically, by engaging first and foremost in mission the fortunes of the church were transformed."[14]

Care of the poor is the mission of God experiencing something approaching full bloom in our wider society. And it is a global mission. If missions is God's yes to the world, then the global outrage at injustice that has now reached unprecedented levels should empower us to become more deeply involved in what God is already doing in His world. Bosch says, "In our time God's yes to the world reveals itself, to a large extent, in the church's missionary engagement in respect of the realities of injustice, oppression, poverty, discrimination and violence."[15]

DEFINITION, NOT ACTIVITY

Perhaps if we want to see integral missions happen more deeply across our Christian cultures we need to enable people to see that the issue of injustice is not one of activity but of definition. And as Gary Haugen suggests, in each era God gives His church an escape "from the suffocating fears, corruption and mediocrity of religion. . . ." Isaiah 58 is that road to recovery.[16]

Today the creation is groaning again: it's groaning about poverty, the environment, and the need for sustainable values. But missions is also important as we develop partnerships with governments that have come to value the role of faith-based activities. The Church Partnership Programme in Australia builds critical relationships with churches in Papua New Guinea. The U.K. government's consultation on faith and development is another active example of creative pro-poor partnership. Gaining government acceptance and funding for our work can so easily neutralize the claims of the gospel. Indeed, a relationship may exist between our proximity to political decision-makers and our ownership of Christian fundamentals. The closer we get to power, for example, the more cautious we can become about the exclusive claims of the Cross. But in Christian partnerships with government, our focus on missions is most likely to preserve our Christian distinctive and make us recognizable to Christians in the pews with whom we wish to strengthen partnerships in the years ahead.

I am intrigued by the project of a theology of development taking place between the Catholic Agency for Overseas Development (CAFOD) and Tearfund. As Chris Bain, CEO of CAFOD conceded, this would have been an unlikely partnership five years ago.[17] And this also appears to be the impetus behind the new initiative of the Anglican Alliance: mapping its development work across the Anglican Communion, promoting South-South relationships and advocacy across its 800 million people as well as building ecumenical relationships to serve the poor. If our partnerships are to be meaningful and sustainable they need to be tested against our understanding of God's mission to the poor already taking place in the world and of which we are an integral part.[18]

EFFECTIVE ADVOCATES, NOT PARTNERSHIP SPECIALISTS

Christian communities are ready as never before to engage in meaningful responses to the poor, but we still have a huge tendency to leave partnerships to the specialists. If we are to enlist many more Christians to become effective advocates we will do so as we convert poverty reduction from a program to God's mission in which Christians already have been implicated as advocates for the poor.

Commitment to excellence in cross-cultural partnerships emerges as a result of experiences on the front line of development over many years. But it must continue to flow from our passion and commitment to global response to poverty and the mission of God.

Summary of Key Points

1. Partner with churches in the South, empowering them to take leadership without feeling the need to defer to the North.

2. Partner with the greater society or culture that often echoes what God leads us to do, as in the case of global concern for the poor—Live Aid concerts, the environment, etc.

3. Develop partnerships with governments who often choose to work with Christian organizations to fufill our missions mandate.

4. Continue to work within the Christian community to address issues of global concern consistent with God's calling to the church.

5. Throughout these partnerships, which may or may not be with other believers, Christians set themselves apart by maintaining a focus on the gospel in word and deed.

SERVANT PARTNERSHIP: THE KEY TO SUCCESS IN CROSS-CULTURAL MINISTRY RELATIONSHIPS

JON LEWIS, PARTNERS INTERNATIONAL

Jon Lewis is the president/CEO of
Partners International, a position he took
in August 2003 after 26 years at Mission
Aviation Fellowship. Jon took the helm
at Partners International during its 60th
year of ministry and focuses on building
on the established foundation, seeking
to grow the organization's position as
the premier agency impacting global
Christian mission through extraordinary
indigenous ministries.

In a time of tremendous dynamic change, the whole context of world missions was shifting. The historic center of missionary-sending endeavors no longer was at the cutting edge of where things happened. Instead, exciting new advances in missions outreach happened from new centers of church growth. Once considered missions frontiers, those very places were mobilizing workers to go out to even newer frontiers. Old paradigms of mission strategy were discarded while new ones were created.

Are we talking about the next Christendom? The current 21st century transition from Global North to the Global South? Nope! Try 1st century church history as recorded in Acts 11–13. A significant rise in persecution, culminating in the martyrdom of Stephen and James and the scattering of the early church mentioned in Acts 12, turned missions in the early church on its head. From that point forward, Jerusalem never again was the center of missionary-sending activity. Instead, Antioch and other frontier areas became the launching pads for a whole new outreach to the Gentiles of Asia Minor.

Without question, we are experiencing a similar paradigm shift in global missions today. The fall of the World Trade Centers in New York City on September 11, 2001, marked a significant change in world outlook toward the West. The event signaled that no longer would the West be the dominant and accepted voice in the world. I believe that moment also perhaps was our "Chapter 12" experience in the missions world, marking the beginning of the end of two centuries in which almost all missionary action had been launched from the West—especially North America. Fortunately, this instructive example from the book of Acts teaches us many lessons on how to navigate the difficult waters that come with any epic shift in global missions strategy. Central to these lessons is a new mindset toward partnership in missions endeavor. Christians in the 1st century needed this mindset, and we need it today as we face tectonic shifts in demographics among God's people worldwide.

NEW MINDSET FO R PARTNERSHIP

Partnering together for missions outreach is certainly nothing new. In Acts 15 we see a wonderful example of dialogue and cooperation as both old and new harvest workers agreed to cooperate in reaching the Gentiles of the day. And partnership was a major theme of Western missions during the past 100 years, with the majority of the effort spent on giving birth to fledgling indigenous churches. But today, as the Global South actually begins to eclipse the Global North in the sheer quantity (and sometimes quality) of Christian impact, we need a different mindset of partnership, one I would like to call *servant partnership*.

Much of our Western understanding of partnership, even in the context of the church, comes from business. Two parties partner for purposes of mutual benefit. If the partnering effort no longer benefits one of the parties, the perceived need for partnership disappears as well.

Servant partnership, on the other hand, does not focus on mutual benefit but on the desire to see a single vision accomplished. In servant partnership one party puts aside personal agendas and invests in the accomplishment of the vision by promoting the calling of the other partner. Servant partnership is to partnership what servant leadership is to leadership. It is a willingness to put aside position, title, status, and even personal benefit in order to serve others and make them successful. Servant leadership is not the only way to lead, and servant partnership is not the only way to partner, but certainly it embodies the biblical values of Philippians 2: "Your attitude should be the same as that of Christ Jesus: Who, being in very nature God, did not consider equality with God something to be grasped, but made himself nothing, taking the very nature of a servant" (Philippians 2:5-7).

One of the clear cries heard today from church leaders in the Global South is that, despite good intentions, most partnership with the Western missions enterprise is not of this kind. Instead, partnerships continue to be based on the business model of mutual benefit or, even worse, on a colonial model with a top-down, paternalistic emphasis. It doesn't help that the so-called partnership "Golden Rule" continues to rear its ugly head: the West still owns most of the "gold" and, therefore, gets to make the rules. Although the West, particularly North America, continues to be the resource-rich, our brothers and sisters in the Global South are increasingly the opportunity-rich. That is why this day calls for a new mindset of collaboration that demands the application of servant partnership.

Although I recently coined this new label, I believe Partners International has sought to embody the principles of servant partnership throughout its 67-year history of ministry service and learned much about what it means to implement servant partnership in cross-cultural relationships. In particular, we grasped that servant partnership must be fleshed out in both *attitude* and *action*.

SERVANT PARTNERSHIP ACTION

In the 1940s and 1950s when our organization was a fledgling mission, the concept of partnering with indigenous organizations, especially to the point of entrusting them with funds for ministry implementation, was revolutionary. However, by 2004, partnership in missions not only became familiar in missions circles, but it was the most important missions strategy applied anywhere. This caused us at Partners International to take some time to rethink what we mean by this overused word— *partnership*. The result was a document we call our "Covenant of Partnership" that outlines six principles of healthy, cross-cultural, missional partnership we seek to follow:

1. Mandate: Partnership is not just a good suggestion, but God's mandate for His church.

2. Mutual: All parties must commit to both give and take.

3. Moving: Partnership is not static but dynamic, and therefore change will happen.

4. Multiple: Partnership will naturally draw in other parties to create ministry networks.

5. Measurable: Measurable accountability provides mutual trust.

6. Messy: Since partnership is based on personal relationships, inevitably meeting the expectations of all parties will be challenging.

Partners International learned, however, that just describing a philosophy of partnership in this covenant was not enough to bridge the divide between Western and non-Western cultures. Nothing can more quickly defeat well-intentioned partnership than confused expectations created by different cultural perspectives. One brilliant attempt at grasping this challenge was offered by our own Alex Araujo at the 2009 Consultation on Support of Indigenous Ministries in his presentation of the powerboat and sailboat metaphor:

> A powerboat captures the essence of the Western paradigm. Power is inside the boat, in the hands of the human operator. The powerboat metaphor represents "taking control." The destination—and getting there fast—is often most important. Unless there is a calamity on the sea such as a catastrophic storm, it [the boat] will go wherever the captain directs.

> Contrast the sailboat, representing the [non-Western]

paradigm of less control. While the people in a sailboat have some control and power, their power is much more subordinate to the wind. Success depends completely on their cooperation with the wind. They respect and carefully assess the context and realize that flexibility is one of their greatest resources. The sailboat epitomizes high trust and less control.

Araujo concludes that to work in greater collaboration with the emerging power-house of the non-Western evangelical church, the West will need to learn how to work with:

- greater mutuality, equality, and vulnerability
- more emphasis on relationship and less on accomplishment
- increased sensitivity to context that overrides the automatic exportation of Western ministry methodology
- higher dependence on God's Spirit and less dominance of Western business practices.

Inculcating these attitudes of servant partnership into the fabric of our ministry has taken a long time, even decades, and is not without difficulties along the way. Nevertheless, we are convinced more than ever that this concept not only must drive the values for which we are known but also is the first step toward any successful cross-cultural ministry relationship we participate in.

SERVANT PARTNERSHIP ACTION

Believing in servant partnership is one thing. Acting it out in practical implementation is another. Today, Partners International is redesigning its role as a catalyst for healthy missions partnerships. Whereas in the past most of our efforts were on funding individual ministry projects and worker sponsorships, today we see our role as helping national leaders accomplish their God-given vision so that they might develop successful ministries with long-term sustainability. Our focus now is on developmental partnership that we define in three distinct phases: (1) discover, (2) grow, and (3) launch. Each of these three phases offers us new opportunities to demonstrate servant partnership in fresh new ways.

Phase 1: Discover

As God actively raises up a whole new generation of non-Western, indigenous ministry leaders with great vision for advancing His kingdom in their corners of the world, we want to be a mission actively involved in discovering who these leaders are. However, as we do so, we find that few have the financial or nonfinancial resources necessary to bring their particular vision to fruition. That is why we actively seek to identify, equip, and help young national leaders get their—not our—dreams off the ground. The discover phase lasts no more than two to three years. During this time, both parties learn if there is both the right commitment and the right chemistry for deeper partnership.

Phase 2: Grow

Once a ministry proves to be a serious partner, Partners International commits to an extended time of investing training, prayer, people, and funds into the national ministry. The intention is to help with organizational and ministry growth. We don't use cookie-cutter approaches. We customize each partnership according to context, relationship, and purpose. One of the key objectives of this phase is to determine together what the right economic model might be for financial sustainability to assure ongoing ministry fulfillment without creating unhealthy dependency. Simultaneously, our hope is to acquaint and introduce the national ministry to a number of other like-minded ministries and churches that can offer customized training or other resources that will help improve ministry strategy and effectiveness.

Phase 3: Launch

Just as a plane launches into the sky when it reaches its airborne velocity, so we too strive for the point at which a national ministry can successfully press forward with sustained accomplishment of its ministry vision. At this point, our partnership involvement changes from being a growth mentor to a network catalyst. Besides providing a conduit for some continued ministry funding, which the national ministry now becomes fully responsible for, we create connections between the ministry and other national churches and organizations for the purpose of cross-fertilization. In this way, we hope to see whole missional movements emerge from multiple indigenous ministries working together on a global partnership scale.

This third phase presses us to act out a whole new dimension of servant partnership. Although we always will have a role as a resource bridge that links U.S. churches, foundations, and individuals to specific ministry projects, we see that more and more of our activity involves introducing national ministries to each other, especially in ways that will help more experienced leaders to mentor the next generation of younger, emerging leaders. Already we have helped experienced Indonesian-Muslim ministry leaders provide training to Chinese church leaders who want to learn how to reach the Islamic people groups in their own country. At another event, we brought Indian and Chinese ministries together to begin strategy dialogue. One of the most interesting connections has been linking a national, indigenous ministry with a veteran American mission. The American missionaries, having recognized that their mission's 100-year-old strategy needed overhauling to be effective in the changing context of the current ministry environment, took the initiative to ask the national ministry for special training.

CONCLUSION

In the book of Acts, Paul's missionary journeys in chapters 13–28 clearly represent a paradigm of missions outreach different from that of chapters 1–11. It is particularly special to read about Paul's encouragement to these frontier churches to provide assistance and aid for fellow Christians back in Jerusalem. What a wonderful example of servant partnership in reverse as second-generation churches showed care and compassion toward the ones that initiated the 1st century's missions movement.

Perhaps the day is coming, sooner than we might think, when we in the West will be the ones in need of partnership from the resource-rich in the Global South. When that day arrives, will it not be a blessing to experience from them the same kind of servant partnership attitude and action they once learned from us?

Summary of Key Points

1. Servant partnership does not focus on mutual benefit but on the desire to see a single vision accomplished.

2. Servant partnership is demonstrated when one party puts aside personal agendas and invests in the accomplishment of the vision by promoting the calling of the other partner.

3. "Covenant of Partnership" outlines six principles of a healthy, cross-cultural, missional partnership: Mandate, Mutual, Moving, Multiple, Measurable, Messy.

4. The West needs to learn how to work with greater mutuality, equality, and vulnerability; more emphasis on relationship and less on accomplishment; increased sensitivity to context that overrides the automatic exportation of Western ministry methodology; and higher dependence on God's Spirit and less dominance of Western business practices.

5. We define developmental partnership in three distinct phases: (1) discover, (2) grow, and (3) launch.

PARTNERSHIP AND PARTICIPATION IN NORTH-SOUTH RELATIONS

STEPHEN TOLLESTRUP, EXECUTIVE DIRECTOR TEAR FUND NZ

Stephen Tollestrup is the executive director of TEAR Fund New Zealand and the director for the World Evangelical Alliance Peace and Reconciliation Initiative. He earned a Bachelor of Theology from Laidlaw College and a postgraduate diploma in trade union studies and organizational development from the University of Auckland. Through NZAID scholarship he studied impact assessment at PRIA (Society for Participatory Research in Asia), an international center in New Delhi for learning and promotion of participation and democratic governance.

This discussion focuses on one important facet of partnership: a mature relationship of respect and empowerment through a commitment to participation. An absolutely central issue is the question of what partnership looks like on a practical level in an unequal economic relationship between the powerful and weak—in other words, a partnership committed to minimizing dependence.

I hope my audience will understand if I don't quote abundantly from Scripture, chapter and verse, to justify my position. Paul's wonderful insight is worth remembering: "For we cannot do anything against the truth, but only for the truth" (2 Corinthians 13:8). Good development principles align well with and are not antagonistic to the Christian goal to see all people set free in Christ. In fact, central to kingdom thinking is the resolution of this worldly tension of power.

TOWARD DEFINING PARTNERSHIP

Partnership is an overused word. The term can mean many things depending on whom you're talking to. It's important to remember that the word carries many and varied expectations for the stakeholders in the relationship. Sometimes I've wondered whether we should substitute another word, such as *collaboration, teamwork, cooperation,* even *joint venture.* Yet I am reluctant to throw out *partnership* because as Christians working in missions and ministry, something about the ideal of partnership resonates deeply within us. Implicitly it speaks about a hope of walking together on a journey. Paul reflects this thought when he speaks of "your partnership in the gospel" (Philippians 1:5).

No matter what term we use to describe this commitment, what is most important is that we talk about something evidenced in a particular form—a respectful and engaged relationship. We come together to achieve a common goal that's mutually agreed upon and important. Partnership is difficult and at times deeply frustrating; it's anxiety-producing, and I think if we're honest in cross-cultural partnerships, both parties must take special care and sensitivity to move it forward.

When managed well, partnership is a rewarding process. Now, I use that word *process* intentionally, because great partnerships have a sense of renewal about them. They allow for progress, for adaptation, and for changing circumstances.

At TEAR Fund NZ we have a set of partnership values. We will not enter into a funding or developmental relationship if those values are absent or weak in the prospective partner. We especially avoid relationships where the object is reduced to a crude conveyor belt for grants. My advice to anyone is to choose your partners well. Once you open an organization to authentic partnerships, an almost irresistible logic will create momentum and move the development process forward. In other words, when I say "authentic partnership" I mean a relationship where all stakeholders have both voice and participation and parties do not compromise these for advantage. Theologically it is biblical in spirit. Once you set that momentum in place, you cannot go back.

It is worth noting and reflecting on the idea that all truly Christian partnerships are not binary, or dialogical.

Instead—and here I use a clumsy word invention—they are *tri-ological,* inviting and orientating to the presence of God. This three-legged stool is the defining characteristic of Christian partnership.

The primary principle for partnership really must be this very simple message: "Do unto others as you would have others do unto you." These words of Christ drive good partnership, good cross-cultural relationships, and good development. The salient question is, "How can we promote mutual respect?"

TAKING PARTNERSHIP FROM THE IDEAL TO THE PRAGMATIC

Practically, how do we ground that, make it tangible? How do we take this ideal of respectful and reciprocal partnership and move forward to its realization?

First of all, we recognize and affirm the capacity, resourcefulness, and intelligence of our partners and the beneficiaries they serve. We go into a development context with a partner exploring together the capacity and resources they already have present. This includes things such as the local church, human capital, goodwill, access to local goods and services, commitment to transformation, and development.

We come alongside partners to explore solutions and strategies together and especially to animate commitment. As Northern or Developed partners—that is, the powerful—we examine ourselves and carefully address any kind of paternalistic sentiments or attitudes. We try to break down the "us" and "them." We try to break down any sense of the "Savior" complex coming in to help the destitute and needy. We're quite challenged by Mother Teresa's statement that "Calcutta is everywhere." In other words, we remind ourselves that everyone, including us, is to one degree or another, whether in Port-au-Prince or Auckland, on a development journey.

As Dietrich Bonhoeffer perceptively noted in *Life Together*, "God doesn't see us as individuals; He sees us as individuals in relationship." That means whether we are considering an individual child, a family, a women's cooperative, a trust bank, a church, or a community, we recognize the presence of powerful and enabling relationships, many with potential for good. Granted, we recognize there are bad relationships in communities, but that is not necessarily the territory of the poor. Together with our partners we try to minimize and address the bad relationships and support and develop the good. We take special care not to disrupt those positive relationships. We want to help those relationships build and gain strength and momentum.

BUILDING CAPACITY AND ACCEPTING SOLIDARITY

That leads us to another deeply important value to TEAR Fund NZ: Solidarity is an asset, indeed the primary asset of poor communities. We take care not to disrupt this asset, but rather we want to maximize and encourage it. When communities realize the energy they have cooperatively, they can accomplish truly transformational change, including community solidarity extending to the church.

In our fast-paced world, anxious as we are to get the "mission accomplished," we often forget the asset of local community and the opportunity to mobilize it. A constructive partnership, and in this instance I am especially speaking of the Northern partner, supports the cooperative harnessing of collective vision and energy. Partners do not disrupt it and supplant it with presupposed solutions not locally examined or discussed.

ASHA, a partner in India, wonderfully exemplifies the value of community-centered solutions and inquiry. ASHA is a community development partner of TEAR Fund NZ established in 1988 in Delhi slums. They had absolutely nothing when first starting out. Using participative methodology they discovered that the slum dwellers were particularly concerned that they had no paved lanes. Instead they had muddy and foul paths where dwellers got infections, faced open drains, and often slipped and fell into the drains. Now this might not be what outsiders would prioritize. Instead they may consider safe water, education, or evangelism as the most important. But when community representatives, considering all the stakeholders, began to discuss their own vision and hope for the future, they first identified the problem of the lanes.

Once the community knew what they wanted, they then considered how to resource the solution. Remember, we are talking about a poor and marginalized community—high illiteracy with only the most basic numeracy, mostly Dalit or caste population groups with little or no income. Needless to say they had almost no currency with local officials. So how did they move forward and create brick lanes that, to be honest, would be the envy of most landscapers in their design layout? They recognized that the solution was the clay beneath their feet. With resolve and a confidence that they had mastered their own challenge, they took shovel to hand and made bricks out of the very earth the slum was built on. That's the power of solidarity latent in the communities we serve.

We also respect voice. We want to listen as well as be heard, and we are very intentional in this. Good communication is key. We ensure good communication with partners by using a number of tools—community groups, leadership councils, village timelines, and focus groups. And on the subject of focus groups we take a great deal of time organizing and supporting the voice of women through their own discrete groups. Women are information-rich, and we neglect them at peril. This is one area where I encourage outside influence, especially if the culture tends to disregard the contribution of women or dismisses their insights.

Partnership requires that we hear the voice of all stakeholders. Whether it is the church or the community, we need to ensure the dialogue is not simply conversations with the powerful in the community. Of note, we found dialogue with women and mothers to be central. This is one of the few areas we at TEAR Fund NZ insist on, because patriarchy is so ingrained, especially in parts the Developing World—and I include the church. The voice of women, so vital, is too often denied or oppressed.

THE IMPORTANCE OF PARTICIPATION

While we respect traditional styles of governments within those frameworks, we do try to urge and move to more democratic ways of cooperation. This is best achieved through supporting processes that encourage participation. Our program partners and the beneficiaries genuinely are active in Tearfund UK programs, in planning, monitoring, and evaluation of development goals, as well as identifying and managing the rising influences and impacts. This leads to empowerment—admittedly another much overworked though nevertheless important concept—as it helps prevent communities from becoming shipwrecked on the rocks of welfare and dependence. Well-facilitated participation on all levels leads to greater project ownership, self-confident beneficiaries, and a community with a greater chance of success as well as sustainability.

Let me be clear: Participation is highly pragmatic rather than idealistic. We use it for a number of logical and practical reasons. First of all, when beneficiaries engage, it influences the development of knowledge and solidarity. Participation is a vital part of an informal education cycle. Communities learn to work and organize in fresh ways, to analyze, to think through, to dream, and to plan. Participation also develops confidence in facing challenges. Once you have gone through a project cycle and you've seen an accomplishment take place, then you have confidence to go to the next step.

Certainly the programs we start with are simple, and then they get more complex. We do not impose these programs on the community. Rather we draw projects from the communities we serve together.

I can tell you one glaring example of imposition. One of our project staff was going down to the south of Ethiopia. One of our mission friends in New Zealand asked if he could check on the use of the wells they had built for their water program. In return they offered a flight down. Once in Ethiopia, our staff member found the bores rusted and in disrepair. He asked, "Hey, how come you're not using the wells?" The answer was a simple, "Well, we were waiting for the guys who put them in to come back and fix them." In other words, they lacked ownership, which led to disinterest. But the story gets even more interesting.

"Why aren't you using them anyway?"

"Well, we don't like those."

"Why not?"

"We don't know where that water's coming from. It's going down that hole into the earth. That's where we bury people, under the ground. What's going on down there? Who or what is making that water?"

It was the old story of good intentions, Western know-how, and impatience. Someone had gone and said, "Hey, you need water," then put water in, with no participation, consultation and agreement—no partnership. So the project, as we say in New Zealand, went belly up.

The other pragmatic thing that participation provides is that the beneficiaries themselves do the heavy lifting. We support them in doing research, base-line studies, planning, and impact assessments based on their own indices for benchmarking. Authentic responsibility, not tokenism, encourages the real development process. The management of the project cycle gets transferred to the church or community. The community now takes that responsibility, conducts the household and base-line surveys, and does a variety of research and reports. They measure and follow how things are going.

Of real importance is the ever-increasing bureaucratic infrastructure required to keep a centralized model expanding. This limits creativity and eventually growth. However, when the Southern partner becomes increasingly independent and sustainable, new and completely unsuspected opportunities turn up for replication of mission and vision at the field level. This frees up energy for the Northern partner to move to new strategic goals, both internally and externally.

CASE STUDY: MAHARASHTRA, INDIA

We work with a tribal group in Maharashtra state, India. These communities are isolated, ignored, and underresourced. They are almost entirely subsistence farmers, hunters, and gatherers working a forest slowly being destroyed by poachers, illegal settlers, and logging. The outcome has been underemployment, poor health, exploitation by traffickers from the sex trade in Mumbai, loan sharks preying on economic needs, cheap labor for wealthy landlords, net migration of children to cities, and a slow disintegration of traditional culture.

Working through its local partner, TEAR Fund NZ established a partnership that emphasized a strong participatory linkage. It used local assessment and evaluation as standard tools. The community clarified and established three fundamental goals. First, they wanted support in developing an independent water source for both potable uses and agriculture. Second, they wanted training on advocacy, strategy, and procedure for access to local government resources and programs. In other words, they felt frustrated and intimidated by local government bureaucracy and needed to have the knowledge that leads to confidence to access local civil authorities. Third, they agreed on the need for increased numeracy and literacy, especially for women. The community deemed numeracy and literacy essential to end exploitation trickery when community members sold products at markets in town or dealt with representatives visiting the villages.

This resulted in a program partnership where together we helped the community brainstorm options to develop a strategy. We helped financially on condition of local management and commitment to accountability in reporting. These included an earthwork dam built by the community with their own labor, as well as harvesting water from rain. Basic but adequate irrigation was introduced to secure year-round crop. Training in advocacy and procedure led to improved engagement with government, and this led to a sudden interest by local authorities in their welfare. Remarkably, the community discovered their rights to guaranteed eight months of paid employment under the scheduled caste and tribal legislation in India. This brought greater community cohesion, reversal of the migration trend, and containment of child-trafficking risks. Attendance at schools for the children is increased. The numeracy and literacy scheme is well-established. Women have substantially increased confidence to deal in exchange at the market.

SOCIAL ANALYSIS, POWER, AND MUTUAL LEARNING

We have a simple but powerful equation for social analysis: the power of A over B is equal to the dependence of B on A. Almost instinctually at this point, we carry this at the front of our minds. We are sharply cognizant of power relationships within the communities we work in. We manage our status power, our knowledge power, our financial leverage in such a way that these elements don't create partner dependence on the one hand, nor do they overtax expectations for the beneficiaries. We want our engagement to have proper and appropriate balance of power. Likewise we work with our community partner to ensure that the values of partnership extend locally outward and that community elites do not monopolize the benefits of development.

With our partners we take the learning process seriously. Together we learn and reflect. In social terms, our praxis is genuine and authentic. Sometimes it helps to remember the term *praxis* is indeed a Christian concept. Translated from Greek to English, it is the title for the book of Acts.

CONCLUSION

Genuine partnership in the Christian sense carries with it something of Pauline body ministry—respect for the parts as well as the whole. This chapter addresses the issues of the stronger partner in the development partnership, the one with the resources, infrastructure, money, and to a limited degree intellectual or professional capital. These assets make intervention, management of the relationship, and the monopolization of strategic goals almost irresistible.

The path of legitimate empowerment is through participation and divestment of control and management of the development process. It ratifies and makes tangible the notion that partners and beneficiaries are capable stakeholders. They possess critical insight and have the capacity, with support, to plan development, monitor progress, and evaluate outcomes.

While this process can take longer, requires greater patience, and lacks some of the expediency and efficiency Northern partners value, it develops the possibility of a stronger and more sustainable long-term outcome.

Learning process is not one-way. We learn together for mutual development. Northern partners who listen and invest trust, regard, and the opportunity for local empowerment can learn much of benefit for themselves from the rich experience of the South.

Summary of Key Points

1. All truly Christian partnerships are not binary; they are

tri-ological, inviting and orientating to the presence of God.

2. Partnership is best achieved through supporting processes that encourage beneficiary participation and ownership.

3. Recognize and affirm the capacity, resourcefulness, and intelligence of the partners we have and beneficiaries they serve. Go into a development context with a partner, exploring together the capacity and resources they already have present.

4. Solidarity is an asset, indeed the primary asset of poor communities. We take care not to disrupt this asset, but rather we want to maximize and encourage. When communities realize the energy they have cooperatively, they can accomplish truly transformational change.

5. Partnership requires that we hear the voice of all stakeholders. Whether it is the church or the community, we need to ensure the dialogue is not simply conversations with the powerful in the community. Of note, we found dialogue with women and mothers are central in conversation.

TRANSFORMATIONAL COMMUNITY DEVELOPMENT: THE CRWRC APPROACH

ANDREW RYSKAMP, CHRISTIAN REFORMED WORLD RELIEF COMMITTEE

Andrew Ryskamp is co-executive director of Christian
Reformed World Relief Committee. He has served with
CRWRC since 1974. His experience in partnerships
includes setting up programs in Bangladesh, the
Philippines, Sierra Leone, and the United States.
CRWRC staff manage partnerships with 105 partners
in more than 30 countries. Currently CRWRC is working
on including constituent churches in Canada and the
United States into this partner mix. As co-executive
director Andrew gives strategic oversight to partnership
standards and to ensuring development principles are
adhered to as constituent churches enter the mix.

I was in Nigeria, about an hour outside of Abuja, under a tree in a village along with the community members. Sitting together were AIDS orphans, others living with HIV/AIDS, and their families. They were sitting around with the community leaders, talking about what they did to begin to transform that community. The orphans told their stories of how they were adopted into some of the families. People living with HIV/AIDS spoke about the "value added" kinds of things they did through microenterprise, which develops small businesses by using community-generating savings plans to make loans. These efforts began to change the community. The community leaders actually put in a satellite dish and did computer training. They used the technology to educate the community on things like HIV/AIDS. I noticed that the pastor conducting the training had a leather case with him. It featured a U.S. Agency for International Development (USAID) symbol, an Association of Evangelical Relief and Development Organizations (AERDO) symbol, and the local HIV/AIDS partner organization symbol. AERDO members had put together a partnership with USAID to fund the training of pastors in those communities to do the training on HIV/AIDS. It reminded me what partnership can be all about—partnership in community, partnership of other organizations, partnership with government resources, but above all I was transformed. I asked the question, "So where is the church in all of this?" They looked at me dumbfounded and said, "We are the church." I was the one who left transformed and had his vision again expanded.

Time and time again I learn I'm the one being transformed when I am in the communities we talk about serving. The

Christian Reformed World Relief Committee board recognized this truth and uses this statement as their "ends policy": "Communities around the world are engaged in transformative ministry that addresses injustice, poverty and disaster in the sustainable framework of God's all encompassing *shalom*." CRWRC is about community transformation in communities hurting with injustice, but we're also about the transformation of our base of supporting churches and individuals. Sometimes we can use the principles we use in hurting communities to transform our community of constituents. With these lessons in mind, what follows is the practical framework CRWRC uses to guide us in our partnership work in communities.

This chapter is based on material CRWRC teams and leadership reviewed. These principles blend our thinking on integrated approaches and transformational development. This perspective shapes the work CRWRC does in communities as well as our own lives.

COMMUNITIES, TRANSFORMATION, AND SUSTAINABILITY

An ends policy states the main purpose of an organization and defines what benefit the organization brings, for whom, and at what cost. CRWRC's global policy focuses on three key words woven together in one concept: *Communities* around the world in circumstances of injustice, poverty, or disaster are *transformed* and improve their situations in *sustainable* ways.

Communities (groups of people sharing factors such as geography, ethnicity, economy, and/or history) will work together toward a common vision or task. Communities are *transforming* when members are discovering true identity in Christ and true vocation as stewards of creation, as evidenced by noticeably better relationships with God, each other, and the environment. Improvements in communities are *sustainable* when they are self-directed and lasting.

CRWRC envisions a world where people experience and extend Christ's compassion and live together in hope as God's *community*.

UNPACKING TRANSFORMATIONAL DEVELOPMENT

The transformation we seek in communities is as deep as the human heart and as broad as the whole range of the human experience in the world God made. We want our approach to faithfully declare that our God reigns; Jesus is Lord over every inch of creation. "From him and through him and to him are all things" (Romans 11:36). We want to do community development that reflects the depth and breadth of the kingdom. CRWRC affirms that God works in us and through us to transform beliefs and actions reflected in redeemed *community* and focused on peace, justice, and righteousness.[1]

Often we talk about integrated approaches in the context of transformation. We think integration as a way to approach the richly textured reality of our work. By integrated approaches we mean a community development process that targets community needs in synergistic ways. For example, if community health is an issue, we might work with the community to discover underlying causes and then design programs to build parenting knowledge and skills, child nutrition, clean water, family savings and income, women's leadership, advocacy for access to government programs, and values formation. The participation of the community in identifying its own assets and setting its own goals for its preferred future is a core integrating element.

In 1998–1999, the Canadian International Development Agency (CIDA) held dialogues with poor participants, civil society leaders, and partner nongovernmental organizations throughout Asia. One of the key findings of the CIDA study, *Enquiry Into Poverty Reduction in Asia: Who Cares for Asia's Poor?* was: "The inter-connectedness of interventions needs to be examined more closely—complex relationships between sectors means that even the best work within one sector has to be a part of a holistic framework to achieve lasting change."[2]

CRWRC looks at communities as a whole. We see people as whole people. We see communities as whole. Our work with communities reflects the needs of the whole to have cohesion, or "integrity," hence integrated approaches for bringing about change at individual, group, and community levels. In practical terms, CRWRC works in multidimensional or integrated approaches. This means our work usually is "multisectoral"— involving more than one of our main sectors: health, agriculture, literacy, and income generation. Typically our work involves as many as possible of these seven key strategies:

- Relief (relief needs handled developmentally)

- Leadership development (a developed leadership)

- Justice (address underlying justice issues)

- Economic Empowerment (economic empowerment happens)

- Evangelism and Discipleship (a growing church base focused on discipleship)

- Environment (making sure to practice and promote approaches that demonstrate stewardship)

- All approaches we use will reflect the overall "dimensions" framework developed later in this chapter.

Of course we recognize that communities are always "in process." At the earlier stages of program or partner development we may see only seeds or roots of a full-orbed transformational approach. The point is that we *do* expect to see those seeds or roots, even in the earliest stages, and we *do* expect to see movement in a transformational direction at every stage.

In addition, we recognize that more than one CRWRC partner or other nongovernmental organizations may work in the community. The total program being implemented in a community, including the other parties CRWRC collaborates with, must be integrated as defined above. For example, if CRWRC, Christian Reformed World Missions, and Food for the Hungry International are working together, then it is possible that single-sector, limited-strategy activities can add up to a multidimensional strategy.

Transformation must be about heart change, and it's got to be comprehensive. It's got to belong to the community; it's got to be embedded in local organizations; it's got to be sustainable. Usually this involves integrated approaches, but integrated approaches are not the same as transformation and do not necessarily indicate that transformational development is happening. The transformation process has seven key dimensions.

- Shared vision

- Sense of community

- Ownership

- Leadership

- Assets, knowledge, and skills

- Ongoing learning

- Spiritual transformation

These seven dimensions are CRWRC's framework for conceptualizing, planning, reporting, and evaluating community transformation. However, we do not impose these categories on communities. (A full presentation of the seven dimensions follows in the next section.)

All of the seven key strategies listed above can and should be seen as strategies within the seven dimensions. As you have noticed, some of CRWRC's key strategies are closely related to or even identical with some of the dimensions. The strategies point us to what CRWRC focuses on in its work. The dimensions help us conceptualize the marks of a transforming community.

LIVING IN THE SEVENTH DIMENSION

"In the beginning was the Word, and the Word was with God, and the Word was God. He was with God in the beginning. Through him all things were made; without him nothing was made that has been made." (John 1:1-3)

"For by him all things were created: things in heaven and on earth, visible and invisible, whether thrones or powers or rulers or authorities; all things were created by him and for him. He is before all things, and in him all things hold together." (Colossians 1:16-17)

"I am the Alpha and the Omega, the First and the Last, the Beginning and the End." (Revelation 22:13)

"Everything comes from him,
Everything happens through him;
Everything ends up in him.
Always glory! Always praise!
Yes. Yes. Yes." (Romans 11:36 *The Message*)

It's all about Jesus; everybody is singing about it. This is the creational good news: Jesus the Savior and king is the beginning and the ending. This is the basic truth we need to know to live in peace and joy in God's world. God's love, His Word—Jesus—began it all, sustains it all, brings it all into coherence, and wraps it all up in one triumphant, restored present to the Father. That is what underlies every other fact we can say or discover about our world, ourselves, and our future.

When communities are in the process of discovering this good news and what it means—well, they are *transformed*. This process of discovering what it means to live out this reality—that is transformational development, CRWRC style. This is the biblical worldview; it underlies what CRWRC does and how we do it. It underlies what we pray for, what we give for, what we plan for, how we evaluate, and how we talk about what we are doing. The more consistent and congruent we are with this view of the world, the more our lives, programs, and organizations reflect biblical reality. The more communities adopt and reflect this view of the world, the more they come to resemble what Jesus intends for His world, and the more transformed they become.

The beliefs, values, and principles of our worldview, which form the interpretive screen on which our goals, judgments, habits, relationships, and actions are based, make all the difference in the world in this process. This is what Michael Bopp calls the "software" that runs our lives. This software shapes communities and cultures. According to Bopp, the life pattern of communities ultimately is rooted in the spirituality of the community.[3]

Remember the CRWRC board's definition cited earlier? *Communities* (groups of people sharing factors such as geography, ethnicity, economy, and/or history) will work together toward a common vision or task. Communities are *transforming* when members are discovering true identity in Christ and true vocation as stewards of creation, as evidenced by noticeably better relationships with God, each other, and the environment. Improvements in communities are *sustainable* when they are self-directed and lasting.

We are talking about the Old Testament word *shalom*, or the New Testament concept of *kingdom*. Transformation means the community moves with increasing awareness and intentionality, motivated by and aiming toward the biblical vision of *shalom*, or the kingdom of Jesus.

What would a transforming community look like? In general we can anticipate:

- Ready testimony about being involved in change the community values.

- An observable process of engaging in learning about core values, spiritual values in the culture, and increasing congruity with a biblical worldview. This includes increasing curiosity about and study of the Bible.

- Increasing formation of groups seeking to discover implications of core spiritual values for their dreams and plans and interested in spreading the benefits outward into the community.

- Evidence of the six dimensions that follow below; things

usually happen in the community that reflect these dimensions.

DIMENSIONS OF THE TRANSFORMATION PROCESS

Dimension 1: Shared Vision

Communities transform when members discover true identity in Christ and true vocation as stewards of creation as evidenced by noticeably better relationships with God, each other, and the environment. A shared vision is a picture of the community at some time in the future, painted in enough detail that people can imagine it and including relationships with God, each other, and the environment.

When the goal is to build a community, a shared vision is not complete unless it meets these characteristics:

- The community identifies, examines, and validates core spiritual values.

- People believe it is possible to reach the vision, but it presents a tension between the desired future and the current situation. This tension inspires people to take action toward reaching the vision.

- It includes a statement about how people want to work with one another in order to achieve their goals and about the values they need to share in order for people to work effectively together.

- The vision is richly detailed and thereby points to a pathway (possible goals, principles, and processes to follow) for action and change.
- People from all walks of life in the community share consensus that comes from dialogue.
- People feel they own the vision because it is built upon individuals' needs, experiences, and aspirations.
- Community members actively take part in making their community a better place to live because the vision inspires them.
- People interpret vision and can tell others about it in a consistent manner.
- It is based on an awareness of an active relationship with God.
- The vision flows from ongoing community dialog in which the community progressively discovers the biblical worldview and adopts it.

Dimension 2: Sense of Community

Sense of community refers to the quality of human relationships that make it possible for people to live and work together in a healthy and sustainable way.

When there is a strong sense of community:

- There is a sense of place and history.

- People do things together and often share ways of doing things in common, such as decision-making, celebrating, or grieving. This helps give the community a shared identity.

- People build relationships on trust, cooperation, shared values, togetherness, and a shared sense of commitment to and responsibility for improving the community.

- There is a climate of encouragement and forgiveness, openness, and welcome.

- Community members feel they are safe, that they have a voice, and that they can make a contribution to the community.

- They also feel cared for, and in return they care for others.

- The community nurtures its people so that they can develop their potential as human beings.

- The community embraces diversity, believing that each person is unique. People believe that differences enrich the strength of the community.

- The community holds a collective sense of fairness and justice. Not only are the disadvantaged cared for and supported, but also the community works with them to change the situation that causes them to be disadvantaged.

- People have an ability to tackle and solve hard issues, reconcile differences, and cope with crises.

- Increasingly people form groups to explore the biblical worldview—its meaning, implications, and claims.

- A local community of believers is vibrant, out-reaching, and acting with stewardship.

Dimension 3: Ownership

Ownership is the active engagement of the hearts and minds of people in improving their own health and well-being. Development comes from within. Without ownership, there will be no development. This means, for example, that if the community is working on a youth issue, youth must have a primary voice in naming the issue, shaping the solutions, making decisions, carrying out the solutions, and evaluating the results. This includes a sense of their own legitimate role in and contribution to the development process.

In order for people to have ownership:

- People must have opportunities for meaningful participation. That is, it must be possible for community members to actually influence the course of events and shape the future.

- A variety of avenues for participation allow

community members to find their own ways of participating. For example, some people may prefer to attend meetings; others may prefer to have private conversations with more visible community members; and others may wish to help with fundraising or event organizing.

- The community recognizes barriers to participation (such as meeting times, transportation, babysitting needs, past hurts, and fear) and makes efforts to remove them.

- The community negotiates an appropriate level of participation. Some activities require the participation of the entire community; others require only a few people.

- Participants have confidence in their own ability to make changes.

- Participants show evidence of increased risk-taking.

- Levels of participation in decision-making and implementation increase.

- People recognize their own contributions to the development process.

- People show evidence of increasing satisfaction in exercising responsibility as an expression of increasing knowledge of a biblical worldview.

Dimension 4: Leadership

Leadership behaviors facilitate the community's learning and action for *shalom*. Leadership emerges from within the community and can be formal (elected officials and people in positions of power) and informal (those who are not in formal positions of power but whose voice is highly regarded).

- Leadership that mobilizes communities toward *shalom* works in these ways:

- Recognizes that all community members need to be heard and works hard to create an environment in which all voices can be heard.

- Acknowledges community and individual achievements.

- Facilitates community consensus building and collaboration, believing that community members can work together to address their own needs.

- Engages others in tackling tough issues and resolving conflicts.

- Takes risks and forges a path for others to follow.

- Offers role models who "make the path" by walking it.

- Provides direction in appropriate ways when needed. (Note that different tasks require different kinds of leadership. For example, taking charge in an emergency is different from making a group decision).

- Understands and articulates the community-development process being undertaken; keeps the "big picture" in mind.

- Recognizes the leadership ability of others and shares leadership when it is most appropriate.

- Fosters the development and emergence of new leaders.

- Recognizes and activates the resources resident in the community.

- Has an increasing sense of being servants to the Jesus of the Bible.

Dimension 5: Assets, Knowledge, and Skills

Assets, knowledge, and skills are the human talents and material goods a community uses to improve health, such as volunteers, buildings and facilities, money, and time. This dimension is about the community's ability to:

- Relate the use of resources, knowledge, and skills to the concepts of identity and vocation in the context of the biblical worldview.

- Identify and access the existing community resources, knowledge, and skills that will help the community achieve its vision for a healthier future.

- Use existing resources, knowledge, and skills in creative ways (for example, using church facilities for a collective kitchen).

- Make decisions about the fair distribution of resources and solve conflicts regarding the distribution of resources.

- Effectively manage and use resources (for example, forming partnerships in order to use resources efficiently).

- Locate and access needed resources, knowledge, and skills that exist outside of the community.

- Recognize that each community member possesses unique and valuable skills, knowledge, gifts, and talents and seek these out when appropriate.

- Identify gaps in skills and knowledge and develop learning plans to fill these gaps; find the means to gain new knowledge and skills (such as funding training programs).

- Ensure equal access to opportunity to gain new knowledge and skills.

- Bring people with different knowledge and skill sets together in a way that builds a creative energy for solving problems and taking action on health goals.

- Follow through on its action plans.

- Achieve concrete, measurable improvements in the community's physical, social, and economic environment that makes it less vulnerable to the effects of disasters and other events.

Dimension 6: Ongoing Learning

Ongoing learning is a process of reflecting upon what happens within a project or a community in order to learn how to be more effective. Ongoing learning also leads to greater self-awareness and community understanding.

- The capacity of ongoing learning shows these characteristics:

- Be accountable to vision, principles, and goals. This means regularly, systematically, and intentionally checking to see how closely actions and results match vision, principles, and goals.

- Ask the questions: What worked? What didn't work? What have we learned from this experience? What should we do differently next time?

- Reflect on community dynamics and the impact they have on the community's ability to work together effectively to improve the health and well-being of all the people.

SHARED STRENGTH

CONCLUSION

For true transformation to occur, communities and the churches that minister in and with those communities need to apply these solid development principles in their missions efforts. Then we will have churches and people working for the physical and spiritual transformation of communities at home and abroad in ways that build justice, dignity, and spiritual growth for everyone.

Summary of Key Points

1. Look at communities as a whole. Work with communities must reflect the needs of the whole. Multisectoral approaches is an important concept for bringing about change at individual, group, and community levels.

2. Communities are always "in process." At the earlier stages of program or partner development we may see only seeds or roots of a full-orbed transformational approach, but the point is that we do expect to see those seeds or roots, even in the earliest stages, and we do expect to see movement in a transformational direction at every stage.

3. Transformation must be about "heart change," and it's got to be comprehensive. It's got to belong to the community; it's got to be embedded in local organizations; it's got to be sustainable.

4. Transformation means the community is moving with increasing awareness and intentionality, motivated by and aiming toward the biblical vision of shalom, or the kingdom of Jesus.

5. Dimensions of transformation in summary:

   - Shared vision
   - Sense of community
   - Ownership
   - Leadership
   - Assets, knowledge, and skills
   - Ongoing learning
   - Spiritual transformation

WHAT'S IN IT FOR YOU?

DANIEL RICKETT, SISTERS IN SERVICE

Daniel Rickett is executive vice president of Sisters in Service (www.sistersinservice.org). Previously he directed research for Geneva Global, served on the faculty of Eastern University, and held leadership roles in Partners International. Dr. Rickett has 25 years experience working with international ministries in organizational and ministry effectiveness. He is the author of *Making Your Partnership Work* (2002) and *Building Strategic Relationships* (2008).

My wife, Michele, and her friend Kay Strom wrote two books together. Their first book, *Daughters of Hope*, remained on InterVarsity's list of Top 50 Best Sellers for four years running. I'd like you to read a story from their second book, *Forgotten Girls: Stories of Hope and Courage* (IVP, 2009).

It was in a garbage dump on the outskirts of Bangalore—India's equivalent of our Silicon Valley—that we caught sight of the smudge-faced little girl picking through piles of trash, searching for anything saleable. Just as she stepped barefoot into a ditch running with raw sewage, she caught sight of us looking at her, and she stopped. We did our best to smile. The little girl stared back, her brown eyes wide.

A rusty safety pin held the front of the girl's ripped blue dress closed. Gesturing to the dress, Kay lamely offered, "That's a pretty color." The Indian teenager with us translated her words.

The raggedy child didn't move, and she never took her eyes off us.

"What do you want to be when you grow up?" Kay blurted with fake cheeriness.

The little girl stared.

Feeling a bit foolish . . . and overwhelmingly sad . . . we bid the little girl good-bye and turned to go. That's when the girl in the pinned-together blue dress spoke . . . but in a voice so soft we almost missed her words.

"I can't be anything," the little girl said.

As you read this story, what happened in your heart? Did the girl in the pinned-together blue dress connect with you, even as she did with me? Perhaps you wanted to join me in somehow shouting across the miles, "No, you are of *infinite* worth. You are *everything* to us and to God." We esteem her because God esteems her most highly. We share the belief that she is made in the image of God, made for His glory, made to enjoy His presence, made for a beautiful and vibrant life. The apostle Paul says she is a "masterpiece," a poem, a song God is writing (Ephesians 2:10 NLT).

If you felt as I did, then we held a common interest. Out of our commonly held interest, we longed to "do something," to "make a difference" in the life of the girl in the pinned-together blue dress and hopefully in the lives of those around her.

SUCCESSFUL PARTNERSHIPS CREATE VALUE

In cross-cultural ministry, partnerships form between ministries for exactly those reasons. Two or more groups come together around a common interest and collaborate to *create tangible value* for someone or some place. For example, imagine collaborating with a national ministry to bring value to the children and families of that Bangalore slum community by working to:

- give basic education to the children.
- teach families nutrition and hygiene.

- provide women with microloans to start small businesses.

- educate community members about the deceitful practices of traffickers.

Successful partnerships create value—they achieve something. Christian ministries might collaborate to create the following types of value:

- People take steps toward faith.

- People become Christians.

- Churches are planted.

- People with HIV/AIDS and their families receive home-based care.

- Children in orphan households receive physical and spiritual care.

- Victims of rape are restored to emotional health.

- Families benefit from higher income.

- New Christians participate in local churches.

- Christian leaders become equipped to teach.

Creating value for someone or some place is the result we desire in cross-cultural ministry. But to deem a *partnership* successful, partners must not only create value *in what they achieve* for someone or some place, but also they must create value in the process of the relationship, *in how they work together*. For instance, ministry partnerships generally value the following characteristics in the relationship:

- mutual trust

- reciprocal accountability

- two-way exchange of information

- clearly articulated goals

- clear delineation of responsibilities

- sense of mutuality, give-and-take

- mutual support and advocacy

- transparency in financial matters

- long-term commitment

Why is creating value vital to successful cross-cultural partnerships? Because people cooperate when they're motivated to do so. At the end of the day, they want to achieve something, they want to have something or become something they otherwise could not have gained or become without the partnership. The more specifically and quantitatively partners can articulate what they want, the greater guidance the collaboration will have.

SUCCESSFUL PARTNERSHIPS ASSESS PERCEPTIONS OF VALUE

Although you and I may be strangers, this little experiment shows the power of a shared vision to bind and achieve. At the core, we hold with our national partner a strongly shared vision to create value for ourselves and for others. But the opposite is also true. An unshared or fragmented vision has the potential to divide a partnership. The farther we move out from our shared vision, the more fragmented our partnership may become. The power of vision to bind or to divide makes it critical for us to hold ongoing discussions with our cross-cultural partners. We must continually assess the value we each hope to create.

Researchers Doz and Hamel (1998) of the Harvard Business School posit that perceptions of value are at the center of collaborative relationships; that is, the success or failure of a partnership hinges on *the partners' perception of the value gained from or lost in the partnership*. Partners are successful when they assess each other's perception of value throughout the duration of the partnership. On an ongoing basis, each partner must clearly understand his own interests and the interests of the partner.

Because people cooperate when it's in their interest to do so, partners who learn to ask, "What's in it for you?" stand a better chance of harnessing the power of partnership. The question works both ways. Each partner-group must say what's in it for that organization. This is the fundamental challenge of partnership: constantly evaluating our partner's interests as well as our own.

So, how do you ask, "What's in it for you?" How do you have the "value conversation" with your partner?

The "Right" Value Conversation . . .

During a conference on cross-cultural ministry partnerships, I was asked to offer questions that could guide partners in a value conversation. I gave it some thought and realized that, although I had questions, they were not suited to dispense widely at a conference. My questions were not one-size-fits-all. They were not general but rather crafted for specific situations with specific people.

Partnership is personal and particular. The questions for which we need answers are immediate and practical. We need to know what our partners think, what they want, what they expect of us, and what they understand about our wants from a partnership.

. . . Matches Your Organizational Claims

Different organizations have the value conversation in different ways.

For instance, in philanthropy, the process by which grants are made involves a certain kind of value-exchange conversation, but it is not a participatory conversation. The grantor asks the candidate a series of questions. If the candidate has all the right answers, then the grant is awarded. If we measure the balance of participation, this process might seem lopsided, but it is a value-exchange conversation nonetheless.

By contrast, appreciative inquiry is another kind of value-exchange conversation. Appreciative inquiry is a highly participatory process whereby the service provider guides members of a community or other beneficiaries of services through a process of creating change for themselves. This lengthy process enables people to not only create the change they want but also to own the change. In the process, the service provider finds out what value they can bring to the community and how. Then they operate at the behest of the community.

A broadly framed covenant, another type of value-exchange conversation, falls in the middle of the balance-of-participation scale.

In our quest to evaluate our partner's interests as well as our own, the value-exchange conversation must be the right type of conversation for what our organization espouses. That is, the type of conversation must match the claims of our organization. For example, the conversation used in making grants is a legitimate value-exchange conversation. But is it the right type of conversation if our organization espouses authentic partnership? In this case, the method of conversation—nonparticipatory—would seem to defy the claim of "authentic partnership."

. . . Matches the Starting Position of the Partnership

The type of value-exchange conversation we employ must fit each situation and partner. The type of conversation also depends on the position from which we begin the partnership. A partnership may begin in one of these three positions:

- One partner promotes his own vision and program.
- One partner adopts the vision and program of the other.
- Together, partners co-create a vision and program.

Those who promote their own vision and program have a highly defined sense of what they want out of the partnership, with little room for variation or conversation. The value conversation is confined by the existing vision and program. Conversely, those who adopt the other partner's vision and program largely confine themselves to the vision and values of the local ministry. The most malleable value-exchange conversation is, however, by partners who co-create a vision and program.

While I could not offer conversation questions to the conference on cross-cultural partnerships, I have since experimented with a conversation that I can offer. As you consider the range of value conversations, identify which type of conversation your organization tends to have and begin to examine the strengths and weaknesses of your approach. Include in your

discovery process one other value-exchange conversation—
the Value Assessment Net.

THE VALUE ASSESSMENT NET

The Value Assessment Net (VAN) follows the "nominal group technique," which is a process groups use to generate and prioritize ideas. This highly participatory activity increases the quality of ideas generated and the effectiveness of group discussions.

By applying that technique to partnerships, the Value Assessment Net leads partners step by step in identifying what value they want to achieve and receive from a partnership or what value they are achieving and receiving from the partnership. Groups may also use the VAN to identify and evaluate value lost over time.

Following the three steps below, each partner-group generates and prioritizes its list of desired ministry results (what value they desire to achieve). In the final step, partner-groups integrate their lists of desired ministry results and form desired-value statements Then the partners together clarify perceptions, negotiate expectations, identify indicators of value, and set priorities for the partnership.

Step 1: Plan for VAN Conversation

In this step, key stakeholders/members of each partner-group meet to prepare for the VAN process. Your group may be your church or missions organization, and your key stakeholders may be leaders and decision makers from your group. Step 1 does not yet include all members of the group.

Discuss and answer the following questions in order to establish common ground before attempting to do so with the partner-group.

1. What is the overarching strategic reason for us to collaborate with a partner? What ministry results or value could we achieve or create with a partner that we could not achieve or create alone?

2. What ministry results or value does our group want to achieve or create?

3. What value do we expect from the process of collaboration?

4. By what indicators will we know whether we are creating our desired value?

5. What do we believe will be the partner-group's answers to these questions?

Step 2: Create the Value Assessment Net

In separate meetings, each partner-group creates its own VAN by working through the following process. This is a high-participation process, with key members of each partner-group contributing and voting.

SHARED STRENGTH

1. Generate individual lists of desired ministry results/ value. A facilitator instructs each member of the group to generate his or her own list of ideas to answer to this question: "What ministry results or value does our group want to achieve or create?" Encourage group members to state each idea in a complete sentence, avoiding single words or phrases to identify value as well as avoiding labels such as "holistic empowerment." Give everyone time to generate a list on paper, without discussion.

The following are examples of desired ministry results or value:

- 100 Christian leaders are equipped to teach.
- 3,000 impoverished women learn how to start microbusinesses with marketable products.
- 200 microenterprise self-help groups are established with at least 2,400 women participating.
- An estimated 6,000 people indirectly benefit from higher income.
- An estimated 60 people are led to Christ.

2. Share all ideas generated. This exercise gives each member the opportunity to contribute ideas, and it provides a written record of all ideas generated.

The facilitator, going around the room, solicits one idea from each member, recording each idea on a flip chart. This process continues around the room until members present all ideas. Someone who runs out of ideas says, "I pass." Members may build on one another's ideas.

3. Discuss ideas generated as a group. The facilitator leads the group in a neutral, thorough discussion of the ideas generated. In this exercise, members can ask for more details or seek clarification of an idea. At the end of the discussion, eliminate duplicate ideas and combine ideas into categories.

4. Members vote to prioritize the ideas. The purpose of this exercise is not to exclude important ideas but to reduce the number of ideas to a workable list by having each member vote for his or her preferred ideas, relative to the original question.

The facilitator counts all the ideas listed and divides that number by 3 (for example, 36 ideas ÷ 3 = 12 votes per member). Each member has 12 adhesive dots to place alongside the priority ideas he or she selects, one dot or vote per idea. The facilitator then ranks the ideas in order of the group's preferences (the idea with the highest number of dots is ranked first in priority and so on). To further reduce the list of ideas to five or six, repeat the voting process, if necessary.

5. Refine the top five or six ideas prioritized by the group. State each idea as a ministry result or value to achieve or create. Then identify indicators of how each result or value might be observed and measured. For each of the top ideas, this exercise answers the question, "By what indicators will we know whether we are creating our desired value?"

Value Assessment NET

Value/Benefit	DESIRED	Actual
RESULTS *Ministry Outcomes*		
RELATIONSHIP *The Character of Collaboration*		

6. List the top five or six refined ideas on the Value Assessment Net. List the top five or six refined ideas on the Value Assessment Net. Diagram the VAN by listing findings in two rows labeled "Results" and "Relationships" and two columns labeled "Desired" and "Actual," as illustrated above.

Step 3: Integrate Each Partner's VAN Into One List

In a joint meeting of both partner-groups, discover and validate how the partnership will create value and for whom. The following is a suggested agenda for this process:

- Take a two-day retreat with key leaders of the partnership.

- Using the VAN, have each partner-group list the desired results or value it wants to achieve or create from the partnership.

- Compare the lists of desired results or value of the partnership.

- Clarify each partner's perception of value, negotiate expectations, and set priorities.

- Identify indicators of results or value and how to observe and measure them.

- Agree on the date for the next value assessment.

THE ULTIMATE VALUE CONVERSATION

When it comes to partnering in the gospel, communion with God is the ultimate value conversation. In partnership as in the Christian life, if we miss communion with God, we miss everything.

At its core, partnership is not a set of covenants, policies, and procedures. These are merely artifacts. Partnership in the gospel is a way of thinking, a way of being supremely modeled in Jesus Christ. Jesus prayed that His disciples would be one as He and the Father are one *so that* the world may believe (John 17:21). Jesus believes the most powerful testimony about Him arises from our communion with Him and with one another.

Communion is more than fellowship. It is *life together* in the sense Dietrich Bonhoeffer wrote about Christian fellowship. Communion is about *being with* one another in the affairs of life and of death. Let me illustrate.

In 1993, I sat by my father for three weeks as he lay dying of cancer. My mother and I took turns staying with him until the last week, when we both stayed with him night and day. We spoke few words, but the message was clear. "I am here. I am with you." Few words are more significant. Few actions convey love as clearly. "I am with you." It is reminiscent of Jesus' promise of authority in Matthew 28:18-20. It echoes the promise of covenant and evokes the hope of fellowship. "I am with you" is a promise made certain by the present. Marriage vows are made of it. Friendships are cemented by it. Communities are formed around it. "I am with you" is the embodiment of communion.

This is the acid test of authentic partnership. You know you have real partnership when you have the mutual sense of "I am with you."

Communion with God and one another creates the richest possible ground for meaningful value conversations. And it is value conversations that make cross-cultural partnership both possible and rewarding.

Summary of Key Points

1. To deem a *partnership* successful, partners must not only create value *in what they achieve* for someone

or some place, but also they must create value in the process of the relationship, *in how they work together*.

2. Vision has the power to bind or to divide, making it critical for us to hold ongoing discussions with our cross-cultural partners. We must continually assess the value we each hope to create.

3. This is the fundamental challenge of partnership: constantly evaluating our partner's interests as well as our own.

4. The Value Assessment Net leads partners step by step in identifying what value they want to achieve and receive from a partnership, or what value they are achieving and receiving from the partnership. Groups may also use the VAN to identify and evaluate value lost over time.

5. When it comes to partnering in the gospel, communion with God is the ultimate value conversation. In partnership as in the Christian life, if we miss communion with God, we miss everything.

Recommended Reading

Austin, J. E. 2000. *The Collaboration Challenge: How Nonprofit and Businesses Succeed Through Strategic Alliances*. San Francisco: Jossey-Bass.

Bonhoeffer, Dietrich, 1954. *Life Together: A Discussion of Christian Fellowship*. San Francisco: Harper Collins.

Doz, Y. L., and G. Hamel. 1998. *Alliance Advantage: The Art of Creating Value Through Partnering.* Boston: Harvard Business School Press.

Spekman, R. E., L. A. Isabella, and T. C. MacAvoy. 2000. *Alliance Competence: Maximizing the Value of Your Partnerships.* New York: Wiley.

CREATING VALUE IN DESIGNING AND MANAGING YOUR PARTNERSHIP

BETH A. BIRMINGHAM, EASTERN UNIVERSITY

Beth Birmingham is an associate professor of leadership and change at Eastern University in Pennsylvania (www.eastern.edu/sld). She has been a designer and manager of nongovernmental organization partnerships focusing on leadership development needs of the NGO sector, including relationships with World Vision International, Habitat for Humanity International, English Language Institute of China and Cornerstone Christian College in Cape Town, South Africa. Dr. Birmingham holds a PhD in Leadership and Change from Antioch University and an MBA in International Economic Development from Eastern University.

"The twenty-first century will be the age of partnerships."[1] The number of partnerships across all sectors that begin world-wide each year is in the tens of thousands.[2] Despite the growth in and need for partnerships, they still fail at an alarming rate. One-third of all partnerships fail in the first two years.[3] Many partnerships fail before ever becoming fully operational. Literature on the subject includes reasons such as difficulties related to measuring costs versus benefits, quantifying some benefits, or demonstrating the value of the partnership to key stakeholders, especially in nonprofit partnerships where profit is not a measurable outcome.[4]

Partnerships in general garner a great deal of enthusiasm in the early stages but also require a significant amount of senior leadership time and organizational resources. After the initial launch phase, however, momentum often diminishes as reality begins to conflict with original expectations. The costs of starting a partnership relate to traveling to the partnership meetings, designing the contract, and orienting and training the staff who will be involved. These costs can be significant, especially the opportunity cost of time spent on partnership work that isn't being spent towards some other ministry effort. Nonprofit organizations often operate with tight finances. Tension over funds may exacerbate conflict about the resources it takes to engage in partnership. The financial strain may be only one of the challenges in the relationship, but financial problems tend to magnify other problems. Partnering organizations tend to overlook other issues in the partnership if the financial goals are met.

RESEARCH METHOD

The purpose of this empirical research is to examine how nonprofit organizations create value from partnerships. For this research, I define *partnership* as a relationship between two or more organizations that is characterized by mutual cooperation and responsibility for achieving a specified goal. I use the term *value creation* to mean the value each organization gains directly from the project they do together. I use the term *value capture* as what the organizations gain indirectly—what one participant in this study called "serendipitous spin-offs"—that accrue to either organization because of the work they've done together.

The study analyzed three different partnerships using these methods: qualitative data from semistructured interviewing at two different points in time, field notes, partnership document review, and an extensive literature review on partnerships in the nonprofit, business, and education sectors. The participants were designers and managers of their organizational partnerships. Findings and recommendations were split between partnership "designers," those engaged at the conceptualization stage of a partnership and who design the project and process of how the organizations will work together; "bridges," those part of the design team but tasked with managing the relationship; and "managers," those tasked with managing the relationship and the project but not involved in the partnership design.

The study examined partnerships between nongovernmental organizations (NGOs) and universities around some

NGO capacity-building need. In the first case the university and the NGO created a partnership to pilot micro savings programs in communities where the NGO was working as well as other communities around the world. The university provided expertise and research in microfinance models to the NGO communities for the purpose of testing and analyzing these models. In the second case, the university and NGO partnered to offer a graduate program in international development that served the training needs of the NGO and was delivered in multiple locations around the world. The last case included a regional branch of an NGO and a university in that country. They partnered to offer a number of academic credentials to community development workers working for the NGO. The focus of the research was not on the projects undertaken but the process of working together.

THE PARTNERSHIP JOURNEY: A SYNTHESIS

As I started this research, my view of partnering was quite limited and focused on two dimensions: value captured and value created. I imagined there was a simple road map to reach these organizational "destinations." What I found on the other side of this research is that the quest for creating and capturing value from partnerships is a journey, the sum of every mile the organizations travel together. The reality is that numerous events along the way create value, and at numerous points along the way partners may lose the opportunity to create value.

The uniqueness of nonprofit organization partnerships is that often they are mission-driven, and this mission heightens a commitment to create something with significant social impact. It also means that passionate people are involved at all stages. They view the work not just as a set of tasks to conduct but as fulfilling the mission for their organizations. This research extends the concept of value into the nonprofit sector and seeks to enhance the ways NGO partnerships can help organizations achieve their missions.

Partnership Design Themes: Destination vs. Journey Orientation

I have observed two approaches to the design of organizational partnerships. One is the idea that launching it is the most important step, and all other details will fall into place once it is designed and begins. In a sense, this is a destination-oriented approach to conceptualizing a partnership. It focuses most on goals the organizations want to achieve, i.e., the end destination. The other approach is the overly planned approach, which tries to anticipate all the issues at the start of the relationship and does not allow room for adjustments as needed. Neither approach is sufficient.

I propose a third approach, what could be called a "journey approach," a balance of both. Partners must spell out clear goals and expectations at the start, including possible exit points when those goals are not met. Then they must clearly designate each organization's tasks and other areas of responsibility.

Last, the partnership needs a process and timeline for formal communication, progress checks, and adjustments. The more clearly partners articulate the expectations, the less likely that not meeting them will cause tension in the relationship.

A number of factors create value in the design and planning phases of partnerships. Those factors include:

- Knowing your organization's need.

- Finding the right partner based on shared vision and values as well as strategic fit.

- Honestly appraising what you can commit to.

- Designing the partnership so that both organizations benefit and knowing how those benefits will be measured.

Partner Selection

Most organizations do not select a partner organization and then create a project or goal. Rather, they have a need or goal they would like to accomplish and then find an organization to help them achieve it in some complementary manner.[5] In this study, the NGOs had communities they wanted to impact, and they found university partners that could create programs to build capacity in their staff for this impact. The universities were willing partners because they each had departments focused on the areas of the NGOs needs.

Historical Relationships. A key element in each of the three partnerships in the study was the existing relationship between the organizations prior to the launch of the partnership. Each organization conceived the idea of forming a partnership after encountering their future partner in a particular context. These original connections created confidence and initial trust between the organizations, and this facilitated their work together.

This initial familiarity with people from each organization accelerated the partnership discussion, thus bypassing the search for a partner and shortening the time normally spent learning about each other's mission, goals, and functions. Parties entered into these arrangements with an established familiarity, credibility, and trust that provided the foundation for the work together. However, while this initial familiarity was helpful in opening the door, it did not necessarily ensure strategic fit between the organizations.

Shared Mission and Culture. Much of the literature identifies the issue of culture clash as a primary reason why alliances fail. Healthy alliances succeed when both organizations understand their own culture and attempt to understand the other's culture and how best to appreciate the differences—or at least minimize conflict surrounding those differences.[6]

Limits of Shared Mission and Culture. Shared mission and similar organizational cultures are strong factors in starting a partnership, but they are only two of a number of factors needed to sustain the partnership through conflict. One of the paradoxes in partnerships is that while organizations must share vision and be willing to be interdependent, if the partnership is to be sustainable its outcomes must satisfy the self-interest of each individual organization as well. Otherwise, organizational commitment will wane over time. In addition to unsatisfied self-interests, uneven levels of commitment and imbalanced power and resources in the relationship eventually will result in conflict despite shared mission and culture.[7] While shared vision was important at the start of the relationships and in seeing the three partnerships through points of tension, it did not substitute for continued value creation in those relationships.

Honest Self-Appraisal

Partnership designers must assess and express the capacity of their organizations and the changing conditions of their industries.[8] This requires transparency and humility not often found between partners who are virtual strangers and who have needs the partnership would satisfy. The historical relationships between the organizations in this study helped in this area. The organizations were familiar with each other and the quality of each other's work from the start. This familiarity served as a catalyst to start working together. Too often organizational representatives enter partnership discussions and present only the best attributes of their organizations, never touching upon weaknesses or organizational idiosyncrasies. Revealing only a partial image of one's organization can elevate expectations to an unreasonable level early in the relationship. Later, when organizational flaws are revealed, conflict erupts. Leaders, together with key stakeholders, must take a realistic look at their capacity to engage in the partnership relationship.

DESIGNING THE PARTNERSHIP FOR VALUE CREATION AND CAPTURE

The heart of value creation is knowing what would lead to the development of organization value as a result of the partnership. "The viability of an alliance depends fundamentally on its ability to create added value for both participants. The more clearly one can define the value expected from a collaboration, the better one can configure the alliance to produce it."[9] The fundamental question is: *What is it that an organization needs from a partner to achieve its organizational goals?* "Partners must share mutually achievable goals although the goals do not have to be the same. It would be unrealistic to expect that partners would share the same goals as each probably has different business objectives and performance targets."[10] In all three partnerships in this study, organizations shared overlapping goals alongside individual goals each organization wanted to attain.

Defining Value Creation

The evidence of value creation and value capture is a key component of this study. Created value and captured value are, at times, difficult to separate and difficult to quantify.[11] For this research, value created from a partnership was defined as benefits or assets that each organization enjoyed as a direct result of the work they did together. Value created is intentional, as often it is the focus of the partnership design and answers the questions: What do we want to get out of the partnership? Why are we engaging in this partnership?

Defining Value Capture

Partnership design often overlooks value capture for a number of reasons. As organizations are busy focusing on their new partners and the intentional goals they want to achieve in the partnership (value created), trying to ascertain what indirect benefits may come to them because of the work may be a bit premature. Raising the idea, however, that the partnership may result in some new, unknown, unexpected benefit for one or both partners would help them recognize it when it happens and give proper credit to the partnership relationship when assessing its success (value measurement). Only when this scope of value broadens to recognize both the value the partnership created and the value each of the organizations is able to capture because of the partnership can an organization truly assess whether it was worth the effort and whether collaborating on the same or a new project in the future would be beneficial. The classification of whether a value from the partnership is either created or captured is not as important as the realization by the participants that the value does, in fact, exist and bears considering when assessing the overall benefits of partnering.

The Role of Contracts and Agreements

According to the partnership literature, organizational leadership tends to focus heavily on the design of an alliance rather than the management of the relationship after it begins. While each of the three partnerships studied had some form of memorandum of agreement, it was interesting to note how infrequently the original contract was mentioned in their interviews. The basic components of a formal agreement should include:

- Vision for the project
- Participants' roles and responsibilities
- Expectations of what value will be created
- How that value will be measured
- Reassessment periods
- Exit strategy
- Financial parameters
- Conflict-resolution measures

Components of an informal or operational agreement might include the above as well as:

- Expectation of value captured for each organization separately
- How and when communication and interaction will occur between partners

PARTNERSHIP MANAGEMENT THEMES: WE MAKE THE ROAD BY WALKING

Rosabeth Moss Kanter cites a study revealing "nearly half the time top management spends on the average joint venture goes into creating it. Another 23 percent goes into developing the plan, and only 8 percent into setting up management systems."[12] The implementation phase is the most difficult phase of any alliance. During this phase leaders discover unrealistic goals and expectations, unequal organizational capacities, and personality conflicts across organizations. During this phase, participants must manage their relationships, making adjustments to both processes and expectations along the way. Themes related to relationship management emerged from the three cases in the following areas: adjustments within their organization to accommodate the partnership, communication surrounding the partnership, the impact of involvement level of participants on perception of partnership strength, and relationship challenges.

Adjustment: How Much Do We Change to Accommodate the Partnership?

Once the partnerships start, inevitably they need adjustments when reality meets expectations.[13] Organizations must adjust the way they work in order to collaborate with another effectively. The level of adjustment impacts their perception of value from a partnership. Partnership literature does not thoroughly address this process of adjusting expectations, but this research shows that it is a significant sticking point in partnership relationships. This study found a correlation between the level of adjustment an organization had to make to accommodate the partner and that organization's expectations of the partnership. The more each organization had to change in order to serve the partnership, the higher the stakes became and the harsher the partnership was judged when it did not meet expectations. Part of this heightened judgment is based on the opportunity cost of maintaining the partnership, i.e., the time spent on the partnership work that isn't being spent towards some other ministry effort; the perceived benefits and real benefits must outweigh the perceived costs for each organization.

The implications of this finding are significant. The organizations involved in a partnership cannot anticipate at the beginning of a relationship all the adjustments their organizations will need to make to accommodate the partnership. The management of the relationship must be an iterative process. When participants perceive an imbalance between investment and return on investment in the relationship, tensions undoubtedly erupt. In order to restore equilibrium, partners need to discuss the issue and seek balance based on the original strategic logic of the partnership design. If this balance is not restored, the partners may decide they can't give any more to the partnership or aren't willing to receive any less from it, and they will end the relationship. In a successful partnership, the restoration of equilibrium occurs regularly in large and small ways in the management of the partnership.

This decision regarding whether or not to invest in adjustments for the partnership also underscores the necessity of having a broad view of the value created and captured by the partnership. Having a broad perspective enables the partners to accept investment imbalances along the way, but these imbalances are not the only basis for determining whether the organizations should continue to work together.

Communication: How, When, How Much?

The partnership literature stresses the importance of open and frequent communication both within an organization and between organizations.[14] The importance of multidirectional formal and informal communication emerged in this study. While some of the partnerships in this study were successful without frequent formal meetings, a great deal of informal communication occurred using e-mail. The literature regarding communication does not delve into the informal communication in partnerships. The importance of informal communication, as evidenced in this study, is that it not only helps the partnership function, but it also deepens the relationships between organizations, which in turn leads to a desire to work together on new initiatives. Informal communication creates a value-creation-reinforcing loop.

Involvement: Keep Your Stakeholders Close

This study uncovered a connection between participants' direct involvement and their perception of partnership strength. When asked about their perception of partnership strength at the second point of interviews (18 months into the study), those stakeholders who were no longer as involved felt the partnership had drifted or ended. While the partnership literature does not discuss the impact of various stakeholders' engagement or disengagement, the leadership and change literature clearly demonstrates the importance of keeping key stakeholders involved in changes occurring within an organization.[15] This study demonstrates that this same concept applies to organizational partnerships.

The emergence of this connection has implications for the communication that occurs both within an organization and between organizations. The greater the need for a stakeholders' support of the partnership for reasons such as budget allocation or other strategic decisions, the more important it is to find a way to keep them engaged in the relationship. Increased involvement of key stakeholders may lead to a more positive perception of the partnership and result in greater support by that key stakeholder. The results of such support vary by organization and the key stakeholder's role within the organization.

An important question for a nonprofit organization is what form of engagement is required. If budgetary constraints do not allow for frequent face-to-face meetings, what is the plan to keep key stakeholders engaged enough to continue to support the partnership and work toward its continuation? One NGO participant noted that not enough information flowed between the organizations and within the organizations, and what did flow was not always helpful. Therefore, to keep key stakeholders engaged and supportive, it is important to include them both in communication and decision-making in the relationship.

Change

Change, both within an organization and in its external environment, can have a damaging effect on organizational relationships.[16] Given the importance of relationship-building within nonprofit partnerships, organizational changes present one of the greatest threats to the continuation of these relationships. Leadership changes within an organization bring potential for new leaders not to share the vision for the partnership or to want to change it. Partnership managers must engage new leaders in the partnership and educate them about the value it provides the organization in order to ensure leadership support and enthusiasm.

Participant-involvement changes are inevitable as original participants disengage and new participants join the initiative. The loss of original participants can have a significant impact in relationship-driven partnerships. So much time, emotion, and history about what has and hasn't worked in the past can be lost when one of the original stakeholders leaves. Remaining participants may have less enthusiasm for continuing the relationship and reduce the number of staff available to perform the work. This finding points to the importance of having multiple stakeholders involved in the design and implementation of the relationships so that the success of the partnership does not rest solely with one or two individuals.

Tension

Each of the tension areas cited in this study were manifestations of a breakdown in one or more of the factors needed for successful partnerships. Communication challenges led to some of the tensions in each of the partnerships. Relationship breakdown or loss of original stakeholder relationships led to other tensions. None of the tension areas was the result of intentional malice on the part of any participant but rather the unintended consequence of an overlooked key partnership factor.

One tactic for addressing tension that did not emerge in the literature or the interviews in this study was the idea of role-playing. The Native American mentor of a colleague once told him that if he wanted to understand the position of another, he needed to "walk a moon in that person's moccasins." While this is similar to the American expression of "walking a mile in someone else's shoes," it is different in that the turn of a moon is a longer period of time—time needed to understand the perspective of another. Though these partnership teams may not have had the "turn of a moon" to spend understanding each other's perspectives, the metaphor may have been helpful for dealing with existing tensions.

One partnership in this study revealed that the more an organization can take on the goals and needs of its partner, the more sensitive it will be to managing the relationship in a way that helps that partner achieve its goals. This may be a critical distinction in the nonprofit sector. Mission is the driver, impact is the motive, and therefore relationships are critical to achieving the goals together. The more participants can see the journey through the lens of their partners, the more likely they are to work together to avoid potential pitfalls. Even when these pitfalls are not avoidable, the deeper relationships that emerge when one "walks a moon in another person's moccasins" will result in a trust between the organizations. Partners will believe that the other is working towards the good of both, not serving only their own interests.

VALUE ASSESSMENT THEMES: WHERE DID THE JOURNEY TAKE US AND HOW DO WE KNOW WE'VE ARRIVED?

A typical paradox in partnerships is that organizations say they value one thing but ultimately assess the partnership based on measuring something else. Partnerships require not only an assessment of the project undertaken together but also the process of the working relationship and the quality of the relationship.

Assessing Value Creation and Capture

"The viability of a partnership depends fundamentally on its ability to create added value for both participants. The more clearly one can define the value expected from a collaboration, the better one can configure the partnership to produce it."[17] What new opportunities can partners take advantage of? What current threats can they mitigate? Value creation and capture are not specific functions within a partnership but rather a process starting with the design of the relationship, moving through relationship management, and leading to assessment of goal accomplishment.

It is easy for designers to think in terms of broad, general goals for the partnership without asking the question, "How will we know it when we reach this goal?" Without establishing metrics, assessing value becomes subjective and depends on what is valuable to a particular participant at a particular point in time. A second problem with not determining success metrics at the start of the partnership is that the participants do not have a clear understanding of what they should look for. In other words, what constitutes value-capture opportunities? Participants who know what to look for can appreciate opportunities when they occur.

The partnership cases in this study had opportunities to create value in every stage, and the steps participants took or did not take at the various stages impacted the value created and the value captured. The organizations were clear on the obvious goals they wanted to accomplish, but at times they did not define who would be responsible for goal achievement. While none of the partnerships planned for the value they would eventually capture, they each were able to capture some value for their organization separate from the relationship. One challenge comes from the fact that at the start of a partnership, organizations may not even recognize all they desire from the relationship let alone develop appropriate measures to assess it. The discussion about potential outcomes for their own organization (value capture) may need to occur early in the relationship, once the general concept of working together forms. This envisioning engages the organizations in dialogue around what they value and what evidence for that value might be. It also will be likely to substantially increase the clarity of goals for everyone involved at that point of the relationship—and hopefully diminish the chance of unrealized expectations.

In the relationships studied, none of the partners measured all of the benefits accrued to them. So while they may have valued a benefit they believed resulted from the partnership, this benefit wasn't necessarily how they measured partnership success. For example, a partnership valued an organization's improved ability to partner, but the organization did not list an increase in partnership activity or new partner requests as a success measure. Less than half of the metrics used to measure the value of these relationships corresponded to what the participants listed as value created. None of the respondents listed any metrics for measuring the value their organizations captured for themselves because of the partnership.

Too Narrow an Assessment Lens

Management thinkers such as Drucker and Kanter contend that partnerships in the nonprofit sector are more strategic and lasting when partners address value-creation needs. While this is evident both in the literature and in the partnership cases in this study, the danger is allowing the assessment pendulum to swing too far in the opposite direction and solely focus on the obvious measures of value creation and capture prevalent in corporate partnerships.

The uniqueness of the social impact mission of most nonprofit partnerships warrants that they use a more holistic lens to assess their value. Value measures need to encompass not only tangible benefits and outcomes but also the bigger mission and transformation of people that occurs in these relational journeys. The partners in this study did create tangible direct and indirect financial and operational value for their organizations. But the act of partnering—the journey itself— also impacted them in ways that cannot be reduced to simple value measurements. Since the focus of the nonprofit sector is positive social impact, a transformation often occurs in the individuals who endeavor together towards it. As Meg Wheatley expresses, "We can't behave as fully human if we believe we are separate."[18]

IMPLICATIONS OF THE STUDY FOR DESIGNERS, BRIDGES, AND MANAGERS OF PARTNERSHIPS

Partnerships create a rich and complex tapestry of relationships within and between organizations. It is not possible to plan for every contingency that might occur as the external environment, organization structures, or financial commitments change. Leading such initiatives is a challenge. A number of lessons, however, come from the literature and the findings of this study that may aid those engaging in nonprofit organizational partnerships.

Designing the Partnership: Recommendations for Partnership Designers and Bridges

Those involved in the design phase of a partnership have the significant responsibility of trying to see into the future to know how the relationship will enhance the organizations' abilities to achieve their own goals. Using the participant labels from this study, designers and bridges need to:

1. **Know what they are in it for.** Designers need to be very clear about what the strategic intention is for engaging in the partnership and hold tight to that intention so it does not get lost as the relationship and the planning evolve.

2. **Be flexible.** While it is important to hold tight to the original vision, it is also important to be open to new and unexpected opportunities that develop from or because of the relationship.

3. **Accurately and honestly assess their own organization's abilities.** While collaborating with another organization can be exciting and the goal can tempt an organization to engage in a partnership, it is critical that partnership designers do not commit to or expect more than their organization's staff can deliver. Designers need to be sure that what they promise is what they can deliver.

4. **Be realistic.** When establishing partnership goals, designers need to be realistic about which ones likely will be accomplished and prioritize so those that are crucial "must haves" receive primary project focus while those that are "nice, but not essential" receive secondary attention.

5. **Establish a rubric for measuring goals.** For each goal, designers should establish an initial rubric that indicates when the goal is achieved. It is also important to celebrate milestones along the way.

6. **Demonstrate concern for both individual and shared goals.** In order for the partnership to work, both

organizations must gain from the relationship. It is important to care about whether one's partner is achieving its goals, as this will impact one's own organization's ability to achieve its goals.

7. **Know the exit points.** As Covey advises,[19] designers need to start with the end in mind. They need to ask the questions: How long is the partnership designed for? What are the exit points if the partnership does not achieved its initial goals? Establishing these end points, or at least discussing them early, alleviates expectations and takes the emotional burden off managers to make difficult termination decisions once the project begins.

Value Creation, Capture and Assessment: Recommendations for Partnership Bridges and Managers

The implementation and management phases of organizational partnerships are the most challenging. Members of an organization who were not part of the relationship design now may be involved in implementing the partnership to achieve the goals that the designers and bridges established. The following recommendations will help those involved in implementing the partnership to achieve its goals:

1. **Use multidirectional communication.** Communication both from the bridge to the designer and also from the bridge to the managers can keep everyone within an organization focused on the partnership goals.

2. Be flexible and open to changes. Changes likely will occur in both the external and internal environments. When the original vision for the partnership does not match the realities the organizations encounter, the partnership plans will need to be adjusted or the partnership terminated.

3. Review the metrics organizations will use to assess the value created and captured from the partnership with all those involved in the day-to-day operations. Adjust those measures based on project realities.

4. Demonstrate concern for both individual and shared goals. Recognize that both organizations must nurture relationship in order to gain from it.

5. Celebrate goal achievement. When the various partnership milestones are achieved, celebrate those accomplishments together.

6. Appreciate what your partners contribute to the initiative. Regardless of the strategic scope in which the partnership was developed, both partners provide something in the relationship that helps the organizations achieve their goals.

Relationship Management: Recommendations for the Partnership Bridges and Managers

The following recommendations will help those involved in managing the partnership to achieve its goals:

1. **Communicate.** Both vertically and horizontally, internally and externally, communication is essential to manage expectations, keep small issues from becoming overblown, and maintain and deepen relationships.

2. **Evaluate the performance of staff** involved in the partnership by including the partners in the assessment.

3. **Address tensions head-on.** When a relationship issue does emerge, address it early and with sensitivity so that it does not impede the work of the partnership. Partnerships often face significant problems because of relationship breakdown.

4. **Develop personal relationships through genuine care and concern.** Deepening relationships within internal and external teams increases the likelihood that the partnership will achieve its goals and develop new initiatives together. It also increases the enjoyment participants feel in the work of the partnership.

CONCLUSION

Is it worth it? I would say a resounding yes! We've high-lighted here the many issues to consider and processes to respect in the art of collaborating. As Christians, we respond to a biblical imperative to work together to serve the poor and the lost—no one person, no one organization can do it alone, nor should they want to. We become fully who we are only in relationship with others. So it is with our institutions; we really are stronger together. As all good development work has taught us, working together in community takes more time and more effort to create inclusive and mutually owned projects, but these have the potential for far greater fruit and greater sustainability for our efforts.

RETHINKING ACCOUNTABILITY IN THE CONTEXT OF TRUE PARTNERSHIP

MATTHEW FROST, TEARFUND, UK

Matthew Frost is chief executive officer of Tearfund and lives in leafy Surrey, England, with his wife, Katharine, and their four young children. Before Tearfund, he worked mainly in finance and strategy and also set up Medair's program in Afghanistan just after the overthrow of the Taliban. He is passionate about seeing the local church transform the lives of poor people in communities across the world.

When I joined Tearfund, we went through a strategy process. I remember coming with a mindset, imported from the commercial world, that was all about making Tearfund bigger. Success is about size and growth and similar stuff. Patiently my colleagues challenged me on this, helping me unlearn this narrow, worldly view of what I and the organization should prioritize. And so my focus shifted from organizational size to a great scrutiny of how we use scarce financial and human resources to have the greatest effect possible on the capability of all players in the fight against injustice and poverty. Thinking long and hard—and creatively—over how we use the resources gifted to us is far more important that getting more of those resources. This way of thinking is far more able to deliver the kind of life transformation we are so passionate to see amidst the lives of those living in great poverty.

In our quest to understand accountability in the context of true partnership, I want to look at two questions. First, what drives change, what drives impact? Second, to whom do we, as Northern nongovernmental organizations (NGOs), feel primarily accountable to, and what are we accountable for?

WHAT DRIVES CHANGE AND IMPACT?

Two worldviews dominate how change and impact happen. The first is what I call a "programmatic results-based" worldview. This worldview dominates our nonprofit sector. In reality we all work this way, whatever our rhetoric might be. Logical frameworks ("logframes") stipulate how inputs translate to activities, how activities result in certain outputs, and how those outputs then deliver positive outcomes for the poor. At one level, we cannot challenge such a logical way of thinking. We put something in one end, and out pops life transformation at the other. Neat, simple, linear, clear, straightforward. That's one worldview. And it typically results in top-down, programmatic, results-based approaches to tackle poverty and injustice. We in the North pull this lever, here, and lives are transformed over there.

In contrast is a complex dynamic worldview. Here we recognize that the factors influencing life transformation of people in poverty are great in number, often unpredictable, often uncontrollable. Factors include the existing capacity of the community, of the local government, of the local church, of other organizations that may be working in the same area. Then we consider natural factors: the natural environment, weather, water availability, and so on. Historical, cultural, and political factors play a role. And as Christ followers we believe God is living and active in our world, transforming lives by the power of the Spirit. This worldview acknowledges that the vast majority of resources required to lift people out of poverty already reside in local people and communities and in the power of the Spirit working directly in people's lives. By implication we must accept that resources flowing from the rich Northern NGO are small in comparison. This worldview underscores the reality that we (the Northern NGO) do not have direct control over the most significant factors with the potential to affect the lives of those living in poverty. In this complex dynamic worldview, we have a very different way of understanding how change happens in the world. It implies we need a little more humility in thinking about our role, our influence. Actually our role is a small one in the grand scheme of things, although—let's be clear—it can be catalytic and a crucial role.

So we have two worldviews that describe how change and impact happen. It is plain that the results-based approach dominates our sector. At Tearfund, I have to put up my hand and admit that much of our work is still shaped by this way of thinking. Results-based management, logical frameworks, programs.

Research has shown that results-based management (plus rigid use of logical frameworks) is not an effective way of managing and reporting most NGOs' performance. Here are 10 reasons why. I've taken these from the work of a friend of mine, Alex Jacobs.[1]

1. Results-based management assumes that social changes can be predicted, controlled, and reduced to a single overarching problem. But they can't.

2. Social results and impact normally lie outside NGOs' control and may take years to emerge. Many other stronger factors influence them. So results cannot be attributed to a specific organisation's work.

3. Logframes tend to assume that a whole community/ organisation shares the same interests. But there are always political issues. Different people have different and conflicting interests. Some people gain while others lose.

4. Logframes tend to focus attention more on a specific NGO's actions and less on the people we're trying to help and their wider context, or other actors' efforts.

5. Initial plans are never completely accurate; local circumstances and priorities change during a project. So plans are not a reliable guide for action. Actions often have unintended consequences not included in an original logframe.

6. Logframes reduce flexibility. So they squeeze out ongoing dialogue with local people and learning/trying different ways of doing things.

7. Some of NGOs' most important goals cannot be easily measured or assessed. Changes may be subjective and intangible (like increases in confidence).

8. Logframes suit decision-makers who work in elite languages using management tools. They do not naturally suit poor, illiterate, or marginalised people.

9. Reports of actual performance compared to logframes are not always reliable and may be hard to verify.

10. Logframes are convenient for donors and senior managers; they can encourage better analysis, but they are generally not used by field staff after initial planning, because they do not fit with how NGO work really happens on the ground.

The thing about logical frameworks is that in principle they seem great; you can't argue with them. The problem is they are not dynamic. If we kept reiterating them, then they'd be fine, but we never do. So what happens with logframes when an organization gets hold of them? Well, then the problems start. We use logframes in ways that create rigidity across organizations. They encourage the false assumption that if we simply deliver what the logframe states, transformation will follow, oblivious to the interplay of the other diverse and dynamic factors listed above. The logframe becomes a rigid black box that panders to the organizational desire for certainty, order, clarity, and control.

Results-based management and logframes have some significant problems. A growing base of research backs this up (e.g., Bakewell & Garbutt, Earle, Ebrahim, Smutylo, Wallace[2]). Logframes do not appear to work very well at all. In contrast, leading development experts make the point again and again that grassroots participation, ownership, and control are essential to sustainable, transforming development. Here are a few quotes that underscore this:

- "An effective development practice accompanies clients through their developmental changes; one-off interventions and pre-designed packages are beside the point. . . . Participation is an end, and not simply a means; the central point of development is to enable people to participate in the governance of their own lives." *Allan Kaplan*[3]

- "Development management . . . is not just a question of getting the task at hand completed by the best means available." *Alan Thomas*[4]

- "NGOs deliver quality work when their work is based on a sensitive and dynamic understanding of beneficiaries' realities; responds to local priorities in a way beneficiaries feel is appropriate; and is judged to be useful by beneficiaries. . . . The quality of an NGO's work is primarily determined by the quality of its relationships with its intended beneficiaries." *Keystone/BOND*[5]

But we all continue to live in the world of logframes, top-down programs, and results-based management, paying only polite and passing lip service to radically participatory approaches. What's going on? Why does the status quo prevail? Here are a few thoughts.

First, results-based management plus logframes are very intellectual, very attractive, very neat, very clear, very persuasive. And, crucially, very convenient to present to donors. Second, donor needs and agendas tend to dominate what NGOs think and do; after all, donors have the money and power. Third, as NGOs we fear losing control. It's easier to be in control; if we do all this complex, empowering, truly participatory stuff, then we're out of control. Fourth, we have not had the creativity and imagination to think of an alternative way to work, manage performance, effect change, play our part in the vastly complex system that shapes change and life transformation.

As a sector we need to find another way to work, another way to operate that understands the dynamism of the world we live in.

TO WHOM DO WE FEEL PRIMARILY ACCOUNTABLE? WHAT ARE WE PRIMARILY ACCOUNTABLE FOR?

To whom are we primarily accountable as Northern NGOs? At Tearfund, we ask ourselves this question. Is it the Northern donor, either institution or individual? Or is it the local NGO we're trying to serve, support, and work through? Is it the local community or the local church that works at the grassroots community level? Or is it people living in poverty? In theory most of us would argue that we should be primarily account-able to those that we are seeking to serve—people living in poverty. Of course we need to be accountable to the donor too. But we must first keep our eyes fixed on those we serve and the communities and the churches that serve them. In prac-tice, is this what we do? At Tearfund we often struggle with this, although we are doing a number of things to try to put this right.

If we're to rethink accountability, we also need to revisit this question: What are we accountable for? Should we as Northern NGOs be held to account for how well we have "delivered" outcomes defined in terms of life transformation? Or should we be held to account for the degree to which we add value to those we directly serve and support next in the complex chain that connects us to those living in poverty?

Our collective efforts are about autonomous development, about helping people help themselves, about development assistance, not development. Participation is an end, not simply a means. It's really worth our remembering that the NGO is seldom (if ever) the most important factor in people's lives.

Perhaps we need to reframe our conceptions of impact. Impact is the value an NGO (such as Tearfund) adds to the efforts of organizations and people it works directly with— those who are one link closer to the reality of grassroots poverty. What contribution do we make? What value do we add? In this way we focus on the factors that are within the NGO's control, within Tearfund's control, rather than on an inflated and unrealistic ability to control a vast host of factors that are, in fact, outside our ability to influence or control.

If we accept this reframed view of impact—of what we should be held to account to deliver—we need to work through some implications. Let me run through a few of these.

First, performance takes place above all else in the interactions between our frontline staff (within our organizations) and the partners/communities/intended beneficiaries we serve. The interaction between Tearfund's frontline staff and our partner organizations in the Majority World (there are 400 of them) is critical. Are these interactions consistently high quality? Do I know this is the case? Am I measuring this? Across all staff throughout the project cycle, do I have a way of assessing the quality of relationships if these are so important? What would an acceptable performance look like?

Second, high-quality work depends on frontline staff making sensitive judgments relevant to each situation. It can't ripple all the way up to the president/CEO. Decision-making has got to stay down where the relationships and understanding and insight are. Do Tearfund frontline staff have the commitment, patience, insights and skills, credibility, and time to work effectively with stakeholders within our 400 partner organizations? How much time do they spend building relationships? Do systems mainly support frontline staff or head-office needs? We've been going through a massive change at Tearfund to try to ensure that all our systems, processes, and head-office staff see their primary role as to serve frontline staff so that they in turn can serve our partner organizations more effectively.

Third, funding claims, proposals, and strategies can undermine frontline interactions if they are not realistic. Short time frames, rigid plans, and inflated expectations can be catastrophic. How realistic are the funding proposals we submit to donors? And receive from partners? How much flexibility does the frontline staff have? How much do they pass on to partners? Are activity plans regularly reviewed?

Fourth, performance can be monitored by systematically checking how much value you actually add to partners/communities/intended beneficiaries. The people we aim to help, whom we directly serve, normally are the best judges of this. We should take a systematic, independent approach to surveying the views of our partner organizations. And we should quantify and compare these results. How have we performed in serving you this year? Is our performance better than last year? Or worse? Is it better than the other funding partners you work with? What's your view? And so on. Then we must act on this rich pool of feedback and insight to improve our performance. This type of systematic survey is absolutely at the heart of the way businesses operate in the commercial world. Not only is the customer consistently surveyed for feedback in any good business, but the very act of purchase (and repeat purchase) is also feedback. We must recreate similar feedback or survey mechanisms so we can know whether we are delivering value.

As we, the Northern NGO, begin to model this hunger for feedback on our performance from those we serve, the partner organizations may learn to do the same to those they serve in the chain—communities and local churches. And, in turn, local groups may then do the same with the ultimate intended beneficiaries—people living in poverty. Wouldn't it be amazing if this happened all the way up and down the chain? Adding value, giving feedback, dynamic learning, and continuous improvement would shape the work we do.

So what do we then show our donors? We show them this aggregated and objective feedback, which surely is a far more convincing, robust, grassroots base of evidence demonstrating impact and transformative outcomes. We have started experimenting with this approach across Tearfund, and the results and insights are exciting.

When I joined Tearfund one document shaped my thinking more than any other. This paper summarized candid, direct feedback from a handful of our partner organizations. Just before I joined, Tearfund had piloted an annual "partner panel." This involved bringing together a dozen of the leaders of our partner organizations for a week so they could grill us about our performance. They gave us direct, clear, actionable, honest feedback about our performance and strategy. We also embed beneficiary accountability into all of our disaster management work, and the feedback we get is powerful stuff. We are now exploring how to get far more systematic partner feedback across all our partner relationships.

Let's be clear; this is difficult. But surely it is also the right thing to do. Acting on the feedback is critical; if we don't do anything about it, we're not going to get feedback again. That means that I have to create an empowered organization. I've got to empower my frontline staff, because feedback they get can't come all the way up to me. No, I've got to give them freedom and flexibility to respond. I've got to let go of more and more power and control to my frontline staff, and this can be unsettling. It is challenging to ensure the feedback is unbiased and objective, but there are ways to do this.

We've also got to challenge institutional donors to rethink accountability and how we engage our supporters. We can no longer claim direct attribution—your money will directly transform so many lives—because that's not the way the system works. We have to start speaking in terms of how our supporters and organizations help unleash the capacity of community and people at the grass roots to help themselves. They did it. Not us. At Tearfund we find ourselves focusing less on direct transformational outcomes and more on the degree to which we have helped build social, relational capital with local churches and communities. The evidence is that when this happens, transformational outcomes do follow.

And the ultimate sign that we, the Northern NGO, have really embraced this new world of accountability will be when our Northern organizations adapt to become less focused on size and scale, on our own efficiency and internal process, on our ability to control the system, on logframes. Instead we must move to an organizational model that is passionate and single-minded in its focus on serving and delivering value to those we serve, our Majority World partner organizations. We will know we arrived when we get really comfortable with the whole notion of giving away power and control, which is the necessary condition of truly participatory approaches that deliver sustainable, locally owned development.

Summary of Key Points

1. We need a little more humility in thinking about our role, our influence. Actually our role is a small one in the grand scheme of things, although it can be catalytic and a crucial role.

2. Research shows that results-based management (plus rigid use of logical frameworks) is not an effective way of managing and reporting most NGOs' performance.

3. We should be primarily accountable to those that we are seeking to serve—people living in poverty. Of course we need to be accountable to the donor too. But we must first keep our eyes fixed on those we serve and the communities and the churches that serve them.

4. Participation is an end, not simply a means. It's really worth our remembering that the NGO is seldom (if ever) the most important factor in people's lives.

5. Perhaps we need to reframe our conceptions of impact. Impact is the value an NGO (such as Tearfund) adds to the efforts of organizations and people it works directly with—those who are one link closer to the reality of grassroots poverty.

AFTERWORD

MINISTRY PARTNERSHIP: IT ALL STARTS WITH YOUR POSTURE

The mechanics of partnerships—factors in finding good partners, designing and contracting good partnerships, managing projects—can be taught. In fact, I actually do teach these things. More challenging to teach is what is most important to the partnership endeavor—the posture of partnering, the posture of the heart as it enters into a relationship with another for a higher purpose. This "posture realignment" happens at the intersection of being challenged with new insights and ideas and immersing in self-reflection and Spirit-led prayer. This requires sacrifice and change—things we humans struggle in doing.

I believe we have a biblical mandate to collaborate, to partner together not only for the transformation of our own lives and ministries, but also for the kingdom mission we've been invited to join. Jesus' posture of ministry was that of the servant, not the dictator. He was the teacher and mentor through parables and example, not the commander. While He had all the power and resources, He chose not to use them for command and control, but instead invited us to be partners with Him in ministry. The models of ministry articulated throughout Scripture demonstrate collaboration: two or more working together, bringing their gifts and talents for the multiplication of the efforts; relationships having more importance than outcomes; sacrifice more importance than success, however that is defined at the time. The power is in the posture of collaboration, not merely the ministry outcomes. In reviewing the compilation of insights and experiences shared in these chapters, three postures emerged that are worth highlighting.

The Posture of "I Need You"

The multitude of organizations not engaging in collaborative work demonstrates our human struggle to adopt this posture, with hand outstretched to another and saying, "Come, let's do this together." As Evelyn and James Whitehead articulate it:

Discussing our interdependence is risky, because the issues involved have emotional weight. Hope and expectation, loyalty and mistrust, affection and devotion, hurt and forgiveness—these topics seem somehow unprofessional. I fear that letting you know that I need something gives you power over me while accepting something from you leaves me in your debt.[1]

In these chapters are stories of those critical conversations in sharing what we need of partnerships so that "my needs" and "your needs" can become "our needs." In my own chapter I highlight the need to "walk a moon in another's moccasins," to take on the burdens of my partner as if they are my own and have my own burdens lightened by them as well. This is a very different paradigm from the traditional measures of ministry success usually focusing solely on "How many people did we serve?", "How few resources did we have to expend doing it?", and "How fast did we get it done?"

The Posture of Humility

So much of our identity is wrapped up in our credentials, our assets and our achievements. With this comes a cloak of power that we wear, often unknowingly. What it communicates to others can be detrimental to relationship. Unintentionally, we let the demands of our work communicate a message of, "If it doesn't work out with you, we'll move on to the next partner to achieve our goals." This attitude overlooks what Matthew Frost highlights in his chapter, that much of what is needed for community transformation resides in the community and we are only one small piece of that transformation process. Adopting this posture of humility is not easy. Stephan Bauman's life-changing event is a powerful illustration of what it takes, recognizing that even with the best of intentions our approach to partnership has an inherent mindset that we are the savior and forgetting that we, too, need saving. Bauman challenges us to look again at our partners as sources of deep friendship, as those who can and want to minister to us and love us for ourselves, not our power or credentials.

The Posture of "I Value You"

A question that emerged in my research and that I raise time and again in conversations about partnerships is two-fold: "Do I value the relationship with my partner more highly than what they can do for me or provide for my organization?" And second, "Do I value what my partner contributes to the relationship as much as I value my own contribution?" Our tendency is to reduce the value of partnerships to the resources and expertise we bring; this is what Western culture values. However, Edouard Lessegue reminds us in his chapter that partnerships must start with solid relationships, and too often those relationships are reduced to the value of the resources one can provide or the tasks one can do for us. Tom and Dee Yaccino characterize this as "a false framework" or belief in the lie that our value is in what we bring to the partnership, not in the relationship itself. Once again, the focus is on relationship.

Surely you can hear the repeating themes even in these few examples I've highlighted. Our hope for this book is to help us all to engage more fully in healthy, kingdom-advancing partnerships, that in the process of partnering, we learn something about kingdom relationship with God and with our partners. The abundance of wisdom and insights shared by the authors contained here is humbling. Behind each lesson learned, behind each action shared, is a servant posture, each servant on his or her own journey with all its struggles and successes. Each servant surrenders these stories and lessons for God's glory. Our hope is that this book provides you with both some practical mechanics and some heartfelt, hard-won insights that will start you on your own journey of posture realignment.

Together we serve Him,

BETH BIRMINGHAM, PHD

Associate Professor of Leadership and Change
Eastern University, Pennsylvania

Releasing children from poverty
Compassion®
in Jesus' name

About Compassion International

Compassion International is a Christian holistic child-development ministry working to release over one million children from poverty. More than 50 years of child-development experience have shaped Compassion's understanding of children and childhood as critically important for individual, family, community and national transformation. Through sponsorship, Compassion connects an individual sponsor with a child to protect and develop that child while simultaneously equipping the sponsor as an informed child advocate. All child-development programs are implemented in partnership with local Christian churches.

The Compassion Difference

- **Christ Centered.** Each child has an opportunity to hear the gospel in an age-appropriate and culturally relevant way.
- **Child Focused.** Engaging each child as a complete person, we protect and nurture each child in all aspects of their growth.
- **Church Based.** We partner with churches — to teach, train and mentor children.
- **Committed to Integrity.** We're dedicated to delivering excellent programs with complete integrity.

Compassion's Mission Statement
Releasing children from poverty in Jesus' name

In response to the Great Commission, Compassion International exists as an advocate for children, to release them from their spiritual, economic, social and physical poverty and enable them to become responsible and fulfilled Christian adults.

NOTES

CHAPTER III:
POWER DIFFERENTIALS IN PARTNERSHIPS:
A CONFESSION AND CALL

STEPHAN BAUMAN, WORLD RELIEF

1. Rowan Williams, "Relating Intelligently to Religion," *Guardian.co.uk* (November 12, 2009): http://www.guardian.co.uk/commentisfree/belief/2009/nov/12/faith-development-rowan-williams.

2. See Corbett and Fikkert's book, *When Helping Hurts* (Chicago: Moody Press, 2009) for a full exposition of this and related themes.

3. 2 Corinthians 8:9

4. I am indebted to Oscar Muriu of Nairobi Chapel, Kenya, for sermons on this and other themes.

5. See, for example, P. Harper and P. L. Metzger, *Exploring*

Ecclesiology: An Evangelical and Ecumenical Introduction (Ada, MI: Brazos Press, 2009).

6. "Ecclesia Semper Reformanda," from David Bosch, *Transforming Mission* (Maryknoll, NY: Orbis, 1991), 387.

7. Tom and Dee Yaccino's "Reframing Everything," rights reserved by www.delcaminoconnection.org, informed this thought.

8. Often characterized as becoming "a voice for the poor."

9. In *Pedagogy of the Oppressed* (New York: Continuum Books, 1990), Paulo Freire refers to this as "conscientization," that is, when the poor move from being mere objects in the process of change to actually becoming subjects, or change agents.

10. Jaykumar Christian tackles this subject by identifying "poverty of being" and "poverty of vocation" as the deepest and worst forms of poverty. See Bryant Myers, *Walking with the Poor* (Maryknoll, NY: Orbis, 1999).

11. The Cambodian government requires registration once a group exceeds 30 people, so from the practical perspective of avoiding the bureaucracy involved, the cells have remained small.

12. Daniel's prayer (Daniel 9:4-19) provides strong precedent for repenting on behalf of others, a "people," or a nation, even when the individual—in this case, Daniel— presumably is not at fault.

CHAPTER IV:
EXCELLENCE IN CROSS-CULTURAL PARTNERSHIPS: POVERTY AND THE MISSION OF GOD

JOEL EDWARDS, MICAH CHALLENGE INTERNATIONAL

1. Stuart Murray, *Church After Christendom* (Carlisle, Cumbria: Paternoster, 2004), 137.

2. Alan Kreider, *The Change of Conversion and the Origin of Christendom* (Valley Forge, PA: Trinity Press, 1999); Richard Fletcher, *The Conversion of Europe from Paganism to Christianity* (New York: HarperCollins, 1997); Rodney Starke, *Rise of Christianity* (San Francisco: HarperOne, 1999).

3. Vinay Samuel, quoted in *Gospel, Culture and Transformation* by Chris Sugden (Oxford: Regnum Books, 2000), 227-228. Sugden's work is a helpful review of Vinay Samuel's work on transformation.

4. Lausanne Covenant, 1974.

5. David Bosch, *Transforming Mission*, 3rd ed. (Maryknoll, NY: Orbis, 1991), 9-10.

6. Genesis 12:3; Isaiah 42:6-7, 56; Joel 2:28-32; Acts 17:24-31

7. Romans 8:18-27

8. Michael Riddell, *Threshold of the Future* (London: Society for Promoting Christian Knowledge, 1998), 118.

9. David Smith, "Evangelicals and Society," in *Transforming the World?*, eds. Jamie Grant and Dewi Hughes (Downers Grove, IL: InterVarsity Press, 1998).

10. Bosch, *Transforming Mission*, 279-280.

11. James 1:27

12. Matthew 5:16

13. Acts 6:1-7

14. Martin Robinson and Dwight Smith, *Invading Secular Space* (Grand Rapids, MI: Kregal, 2003), 73.

15. Bosch, *Transforming Mission*, 10.

16. Gary Haugen, *Just Courage* (Downers Grove, IL: InterVarsity Press, 2008), 40.

17. Chris Bain, meeting with author, August 21, 2009.

18. Rev. Rachel Carnegie, Archbishop of Canterbury's Secretary for International Development, meeting with author, August 27, 2009.

CHAPTER VI:
PARTNERSHIP AND PARTICIPATION IN NORTH-SOUTH RELATIONS

STEPHEN TOLLESTRUP, EXECUTIVE DIRECTOR TEAR FUND NZ

1. Dietrich Bonhoeffer, *Life Together* (New York: Harper Row, 1954).

CHAPTER VII:
TRANSFORMATIONAL COMMUNITY DEVELOPMENT
ANDREW RYSKAMP, CRWRC

1. Christian Reformed World Missions/CRWRC statement of common commitment to "transformational development" at the joint field leaders meetings, Ancaster, ON, Canada, April 2002.

2. "Enquiry Into Poverty Reduction in Asia: Who Cares for Asia's Poor?" *Canadian International Development Agency* (1999): 5.

3. Michael and Judy Bopp, *Recreating the World: A Practical Guide to Building Sustainable Communities* (Cochrane, Canada: Four Winds Press, 2001).

CHAPTER IX:
CREATING VALUE IN DESIGNING AND MANAGING YOUR PARTNERSHIP
BETH BIRMINGHAM, EASTERN UNIVERSITY

1. J. E. Austin, *Collaboration Challenge: How Non-Profits and Businesses Succeed Through Strategic Alliances* (Dorchester, MA: Jossey-Bass, 2000), 1.

2. R.E. Spekman, L.A. Isabella, and T.C. MacAvoy, *Alliance Competence: Maximizing the Value of Your Partnerships* (New York: Wiley, 2000), 1.

3. W. Bergquist, J. Betwee, and D. Meuel, *Building Strategic Relationships: How to Extend Your Organization's Reach Through Partnerships, Alliances and Joint Ventures.* (San Francisco: Jossey-Bass. 1995), 246.

4. Austin, *Collaboration Challenge*; Doz, Y.L. and G. Hamel, *Alliance Advantage: The Art of Creating Value Through Partnering* (Boston: Harvard Business School Press, 1998), 316.

5. Bergquist, Betwee, and Meuel, *Building Strategic Relationships*; Doz, Y.L. and G. Hamel, *Alliance Advantage*, 316; Yves L. Doz, Paul M. Olk, and P.S. Ring, "Formation processes of R&D consortia: Which path to take? Where does it lead?" *Strategic Management Journal*, 21 no. 3 (2000): 239-266.

6. Austin, *Collaboration Challenge*; Bergquist, Betwee, and Meuel, *Building Strategic Relationships*; Doz and Hamel, *Alliance Advantage*; Peasant Kale, Jeffrey Dyer and Harbor Singh, "Alliance capability, stock market response, and long-term alliance success: The role of the alliance function," *Strategic Management Journal*, 23 no. 8 (2002): 747-767; Daniel Rickett, *Making Your Partnership Work* (Enumclaw, WA: Winepress Publishing, 2002), 167.

7. Doz and Hamel, *Alliance Advantage*; Rosabeth M. Kanter, *When Giants Learn to Dance: Mastering the Challenge of Strategy, Management, and Careers in the 1990s* (New

York: Simon and Schuster, 1989), 415; Paul W. Mattessich, Marta Murray-Close, and Barbara Monsey, *Collaboration: What Makes It Work, a Review of Research Literature on Factors Influencing Successful Collaboration*, 2nd ed. (Saint Paul, MN: Amherst H. Wilder Foundation, 2001), 82.

8. Rosabeth M. Kanter, *On the Frontiers of Management* (Boston, MA: Harvard Business School Press, 1997), xiii, 306.

9. Austin, *Collaboration Challenge*, 89.

10. Spekman, Isabella, and MacAvoy, *Alliance Competence*, 43.

11. Doz and Hamel, *Alliance Advantage*.

12. Kanter, *When Giants Learn to Dance*, 167.

13. Doz and Hamel, *Alliance Advantage*.

14. Bergquist, Betwee, Meuel, *Building Strategic Relationships*; Kanter, *On the Frontiers of Management*; P. Karasoff, *Collaborative Partnerships: A Review of the Literature*, in *Profiles in Collaboration* (Technical Assistance Center for Professional Development Partnerships: Washington, D.C., 1998); Mattessich, Murray-Close, and Monsey, *Collaboration: What Makes It Work*; Spekman, Isabella, and MacAvoy, *Alliance Competence*.

15. John P. Kotter, *Leading Change* (Boston, MA: Harvard Business School Press, 1996), 187.

16. Doz and Hamel, *Alliance Advantage*; Spekman, Isabella, and MacAvoy, *Alliance Competence*.

17. Austin, *Collaboration Challenge*, 89.

18. Meg J. Wheatley, *Turning to one another: Simple conversations to restore hope to the future* (San Francisco, CA: Berrett-Koehler Publishers, 2002), 115.

19. Stephen Covey, *The Seven Habits of Highly Effective People* (New York: Fireside Books, 1990).

CHAPTER X:
RETHINKING ACCOUNTABILITY IN THE CONTEXT OF TRUE PARTNERSHIP
MATTHEW FROST, TEARFUND UK

1. Alex Jacobs and Robyn Wilford, "Putting new approaches to NGO accountability into action," Development's Futures Conference (2007).

2. Oliver Bakewell and Anne Garbutt, "The use and abuse of the logical framework approach," SIDA (2005).

   Lucy Earle, "Lost in the matrix: the logframe and the local picture," INTRAC Research Department (2003).

   Lucy Earle, ed., *Creativity and Constraint: Grassroots monitoring and evaluation and the international aid arena* (Oxford: INTRAC, 2004).

   Alnoor Ebrahim, *NGOs and Organizational Change* (Cambridge: Cambridge University Press, 2003).

Alnoor Ebrahim, "Accountability in Practice: Mechanisms for NGOs," *World Development* 31, no. 5 (2003): 813-829.

Terry Smutylo, "Crouching impact, hidden attribution: overcoming threats to learning in developmental programs," *International Development Research Centre* (May 2001).

Tina Wallace, *The aid chain: Coercion and commitment in development NGOs* (UK: Practical Action Publishing, 2006).

3. Allan Kaplan, "The development of capacity," UN Non-governmental Liaison Service (1998).

4. Alan Thomas, "What makes good development management?" *Development in Practice* 9, no. 1-2 (1999).

5. BOND, *A BOND Approach to Quality in Non-Governmental Organisations: Putting Beneficiaries First* (2006), http://

AFTERWORD

BETH BIRMINGHAM, EASTERN UNIVERSITY

1. Evelyn and James Whitehead, *The Promise of Partnership: A Model for Collaborative Ministry* (San Francisco: Harper San Francisco, 1993), 157.